Transition
from
Steam

Transition
from
Steam

Colonel H.C.B.Rogers OBE

LONDON
IAN ALLAN LTD

First published 1980

ISBN 0 7110 1014 5

Published by Ian Allan Ltd, Shepperton, Surrey,
and printed by Ian Allan Printing Ltd at their
works at Coombelands in Runnymede, England.

To my Wife
who still prefers to sit
in a railway carriage
facing the engine

Acknowledgements

I am very fortunate in that, during the last period of steam
construction and the formative years of transition to other
types of motive power, the appointment of Chief
Mechanical Engineer, or its equivalent, was held in
succession by three of my friends. They are Mr R. A. Riddles, CBE, FIMechE, Mr R. C. Bond, FICE, FIMechE,
and Mr J. F. Harrison, OBE, FIMechE. Without their
help and their knowledge of events during this crucial
period of railway history, this book could not have been
written. No other persons have exercised so great an influence on the present day operation of British Railways. I
owe much, too, to another friend, Mr T. C. B. Miller,
FIMechE, who was CME, British Railways, from 1968 to
1971, and had much experience of the practical
difficulties of transition from the time when he was
CM&EE Eastern Region. Finally, Mr R. G. Jarvis,
FIMechE, has kindly given me a most interesting account
of his work in the rebuilding of the Bulleid Pacifics and
has provided me with invaluable information on a number
of technical matters with which he was concerned. Lastly
I must mention Mr Michael Harris of my publishers who
suggested this book in the first place, and who has provided invaluable comment and suggestions during its progress.

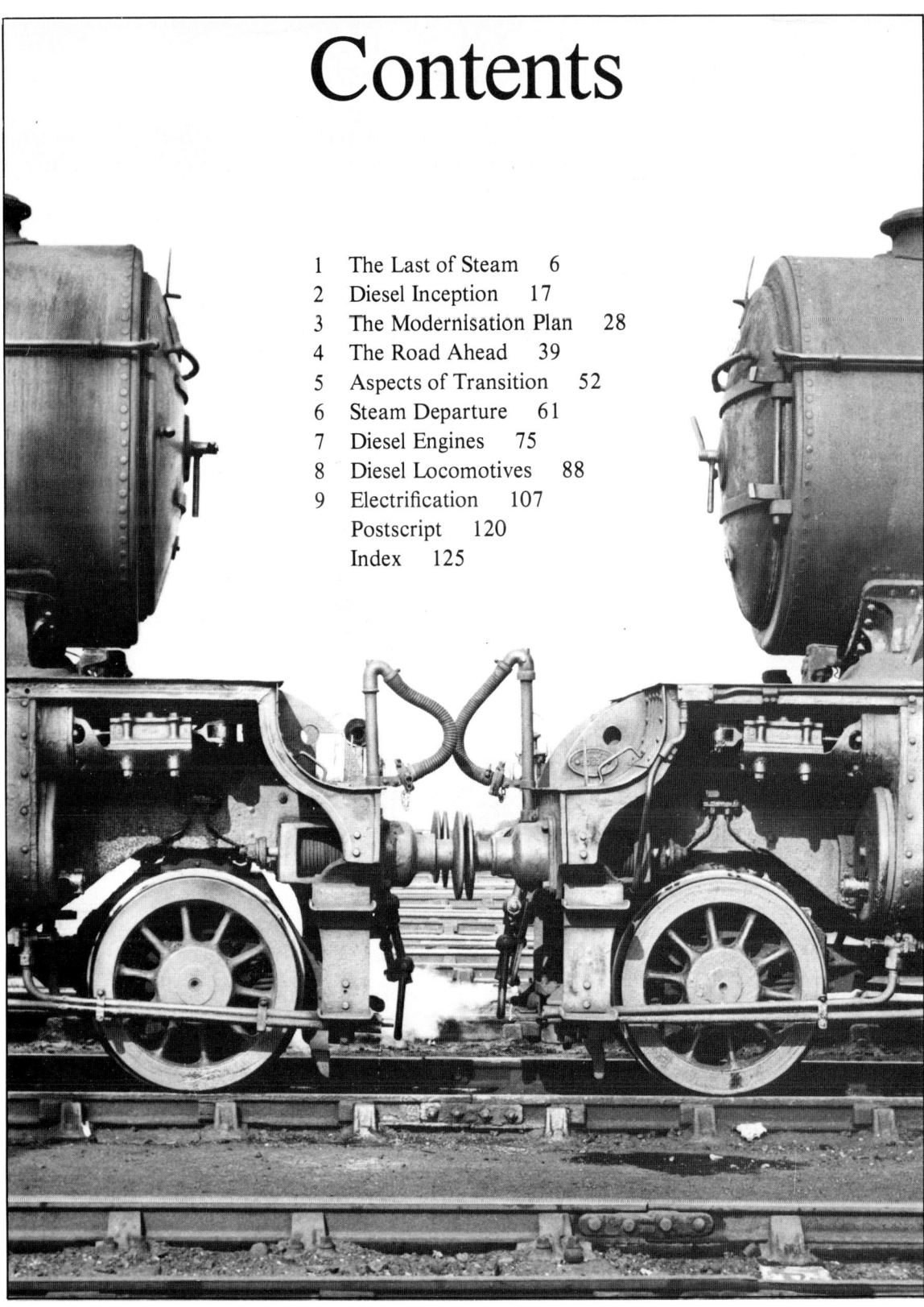

Contents

1
The Last of Steam

On 1 January 1948 the four main line railway companies were nationalised and placed under the control of the British Transport Commission, the Chairman of which was Sir Cyril (later Lord) Hurcomb. The various activities for which the new Commission was responsible were managed by public bodies called Executives. Of these, the Railway Executive had charge of all the railways previously owned by the main line companies. The Chairman of the Railway Executive was Sir Eustace Missenden, late General Manager of the Southern Railway, and there were six other full time members. One of these was Mr R. A. Riddles, late Vice-President for Engineering of the London Midland & Scottish Railway. He had been offered the appointment of Member of the Railway Executive for Mechancial and Electrical Engineering by the Minister of Transport and had accepted it. It was a job roughly comparable to the post of Chief Mechanical Engineer on one of the old companies.

One of the many important matters on which a decision would have to be made was the type of motive power needed for the new British Railways. There were three possibilities: steam, which was at that time predominant in Great Britain; electric, represented mainly by the third-rail system on the extensive short-distance network of the former Southern Railway; and diesel, which was so far confined principally to a number of useful shunting locomotives and one new main line locomotive built by the LMS, which was soon to be joined by a sister.

But if diesel power had as yet made little impact in the United Kingdom, it had made enormous strides in the United States. There had been the 'Zephyr' series of fast diesel trains in the 1930s, the first diesel-electric passenger locomotives of 1935 onwards, and then the four-unit freight locomotive of 1939 which made diesel conquest of the railways possible. In 1941 the United States War Production Board banned the construction of passenger locomotives for the duration of the war. Freight diesels were increasingly demanded and production of steam engines declined rapidly. Of the latter, only 326 were built in 1944 and by 1950 the total had sunk to 12. Enthusiasts for the diesel claimed that although the economic life of a diesel locomotive was not more than 15 years, or about half that of a steam locomotive, during that life it produced about three times as much work as the latter, and that, with no fire to clean and no boiler to wash out, it could give six and a half days work out of seven. This calculation, however, ignored days out of service due to breakdown of the diesel's more complicated mechanism. A factor that particularly favoured diesel traction in the United States lay in the great areas where water was short and steam locomotives had to haul a lot of extra water with consequent reduction in the useful payload. This was not, of course, a factor that had to be taken into account in Great Britain.

Most railway engineers would probably agree that electricity provides the ideal system of traction; but against its many advantages there is the high cost of electrifying lines. In countries like Great Britain, without abundant water power or very mountainous routes, a certain density of traffic is needed to ensure an adequate return on the high capital cost.

Practically there is little to choose between any accepted form of railway motive power, because a like value of power in any of these forms will result in a comparable output in both loads and speeds. But economically they are not equal, and it is an extremely difficult and complex matter to determine the true cost of each. On the prices current in 1950 certain comparative costs of different forms of power were calculated as follows:

Type	Capital cost	Starting te,lb	Cost per lb of te	1hr dbhp	Cost per dbhp
Class 5 4-6-0	£16,000	26,120	£0-12-3	1,200	£13-6-0
1,600hp DE	£78,200	41,400	£1-17-9	1,200	£65-0-0
1,500v CC Elec	£37,400	45,000	£0-16-8	2,120	£17-12-10

On the above basis steam came out an easy winner, with the electric locomotive second. Of course the above calculation does not tell the whole story. It does not take account, for instance, of the greater availability of diesel and electric locomotives and assumes a one-for-one replacement of steam locomotives; nor does it include the cost of electrifying a route. On the other hand, money can be spent on steam without exceptional capital investment at any one time; and although the thermal efficiency of steam is low, actual fuel costs per drawbar horsepower do not rank very high in the total relative costs. In addition, substantial mechanical developments were still being introduced in 1951 to reduce the costs of the steam locomotive and increase its availability.

Like many others Sir Cyril Hurcomb had been thinking about the possibilities of diesel and electric traction as an alternative to steam. He mentioned this at a meeting, and Riddles, who was far too busy to want to undertake an investigation himself, suggested the setting up of a committee. Hurcomb accepted this and in April 1948 he wrote to Sir Eustace Missenden, saying that the technical capabilities of these forms of traction were now fairly well appreciated and proposing that a committee should be set up to review the question of motive power on economic grounds, and that it should not include any engineers. The Executive thereupon appointed a committee consisting of two operating officers, an administrative officer, and an accountant. It held its first meeting at the end of 1948, but for various reasons did not submit a report until 1951. (Hurcomb, who was also Chairman of the Electricity Authority, became impatient at waiting for the Committee's report, and at another meeting, looking straight at Riddles, he asked when he was going to have it. Riddles replied that the report was nothing to do with him, and added: 'In any case, you know that the only alternative form of traction is electrification, and you say that we cannot afford it; so what are we worrying about?')

Riddles, though in favour of diesel shunters and diesel trains for local and branch line services, was strongly opposed to main line diesel traction. Not that he was opposed to main line diesels as such, but because he believed that the main lines should be electrified and was convinced that the introduction of diesels as an intermediate step would prove so expensive as to delay electrification for many years. This is in fact what happened. There was, too, no demand for diesels from the operators; in fact they did not want them. No immediate electrification was possible because of the terms in a Government White Paper on capital investment. On 1 January 1948, therefore, there was really no practicable alternative to continuing with steam traction on the main lines. Riddles, indeed, says that there was no pressure put on him by the Transport Commission to substitute diesels for steam in his traction plans, nor did he get the impression that any diesel lobby was putting pressure on the Government to adopt this form of motive power.

Owing to the war and the difficult years that followed it there had been no adequate replacement of locomotives, and many of those in use were suffering from old age or lack of maintenance. There was an urgent need, then, for new locomotives, but what should be built presented something of a problem. One method would have been for the various Regions to have carried on development and construction in accordance with the practice and policies of the former main line companies, and there were some very vocal advocates for that solution. But the result would have been that for each traffic purpose four different kinds of locomotive would have been produced, and these would have been different in every component, made of materials having different specifications for the same purpose, and restricted in some cases by weight and loading gauge to the lines of the Region of their origin. A second method would have been to select the designs of one of the former companies as the standard for British Railways. Riddles rejected this because the products of each of the former companies had reached a high standard of development and no one company was indisputably pre-eminent. There remained two other possibilities: one was to nominate for each traffic category the best of an existing type for all future construction, and the other to develop a completely new range of standard designs.

On 8 January, therefore, Riddles set up a policy committee to make recommendations covering firstly the stan-

dardisation of fittings and equipment, and secondly the possibility of selecting in each traffic category the best existing Regional type. In addition he arranged to have trials of different express passenger, mixed traffic, and heavy freight locomotives, running on various lines of the different Regions.

The trials showed that no one Regional type was so superior to the others as to be an obvious selection for standard production; and this was endorsed by the Locomotive Standards Committee, who also found the margin between different Regions so close that they were unable to recommend the adoption of any one type in each category. As regards fittings, though a wide range could be standardised on new locomotives they would entail considerable alterations if used on existing engines. A further difficulty was the strong Regional objection to any locomotive or fitting imported from another region.

Riddles came to the conclusion, therefore, that he would have to develop a series of new engines. This decision raised two more problems; firstly the kind of engines that were needed, and secondly the method to be used in their design and construction. The postwar circumstances demanded engines which, though incorporating all that was best in modern practice, should be simple to drive, easy to maintain, and able to run with indifferent fuel. He decided that in the higher power range his engines would be of entirely new design. In the lower power range, however, the LMS alone among the former companies had produced three classes which embodied every modern feature. They had proved very successful and could run over most routes in the country. As they had no competitors there could not be the same objection by other Regions to using them. They were therefore included, with only detail modification, in the standard range.

As regards design and construction, one difficulty was that Riddles had no Chief Draughtsman, and not one drawing office but four. Chief draughtsmen were men of long and varied experience who translated their CME's instructions into fact and even, on occasions, told CMEs why their ideas were impracticable. Riddles got over this difficulty in a most ingenious way by establishing a sort of corporate chief draughtsman. He formed the chief draughtsmen of Derby, Swindon, Doncaster, and Brighton into a body under the chairmanship of E.S. Cox, whom he brought from the LMS and appointed Executive Officer, Design.

For the various activities which came under him, Riddles appointed three chief officers: R.C. Bond (LMS) for locomotive construction and maintenance; C.M. Cock (Southern) for electrical engineering, and E. Pugson (LMS) for carriage and wagon construction. Electric and diesel-electric locomotives were in Cock's department, but diesel locomotives with non-electric transmission were Bond's responsiblity. The Chief Officer for motive power, H. Rudgard (LMS) was responsible jointly to Riddles and to V.M. Barrington-Ward (LNER), the Operating Member.

Amongst the principles that Riddles laid down for his engines were that they should have the greatest steam-producing capacity that weight and dimensions permitted;

that all working parts should be simple, visible, and get-at-able; and that each class should be able to work mixed traffic over the widest possible range. Standard fittings were to be used for all engines, and only two cylinders were to be used where they would suffice for the job, and these and their valve gear were to be outside. Wide fireboxes were to be incorporated where practicable to obtain good steaming with poor coal, to raise the maximum steam production, and to lower the rate of combustion. A minor, but essential psychological, point was that there should be a family resemblance between all the engines, and that they should resemble those of any one Region as little as possible (though there was inevitably, with the above design factors, a closer visual affinity to the later engines of the LMS than to those of any of the other former companies.)

Studies led to the conclusion that 12 different locomotive types would meet all the requirements of British Railways. It was obviously desirable that the complete design for each of these should be allocated to one drawing office; but this in itself could lead to perhaps unintentional perpetuation of previous company practice. To avoid this Riddles decided to give each drawing office a dual role: to be parent to one or more locomotive types and to design components for all types. Thus, Derby was parent to the two classes of Pacifics and was to design bogies and trucks, wheels, axles, and axleboxes.

The top passenger range was covered adequately for the time being by the 'Duchesses', A4s, 'Kings', and 'Merchant Navys' of the old companies. The immediate need was for a passenger engine of some 30,000 to 35,000lb tractive effort. This was met by a Class 7 Pacific with a taper boiler of 6ft 5$\frac{1}{2}$in diameter at the throat plate and 250lb/in² pressure, which was intended to do the work of, for instance, a rebuilt LMS 'Royal Scot' or a Great Western 'Castle'. There was also a Class 6 Pacific, to work over routes where axle load restrictions prohibited the use of the Class 7. For general mixed traffic duties there was a Class 5 4-6-0 with the boiler of the LMS Class 5 and intended for similar duties, but modified slightly and with a slightly heavier axle load than the Class 6.

Axle load was not the only restriction on locomotives. In 1949 two constructional gauges, L1 and L2, were established, of which the former, and smaller, was designed to fit the loading gauge of any line in Great Britain, whilst the latter permitted movement over nearly all the main lines. It was decided that locomotives of Class 4 and below should be allowed to run on any line that their axle weight allowed, whilst Class 5 and upwards need only conform to the L2 construction gauge.

There were three locomotive types in the Class 4 category: a 2-6-4 tank engine, a 4-6-0, and a 2-6-0. The tank engine was developed from the very similar LMS 2-6-4T, but to enable it to pass the L1 construction gauge the cylinders were reduced in size and, to obtain the same power, the boiler pressure was increased. The Class 4 4-6-0 was a tender version of the 2-6-4T for longer distance runs on L1 gauge railways. As there was no bogie at the trailing end, however, Riddles considered that one at the front would give better guiding than a pony truck. The 2-

6-0 was Ivatt's freight engine for the LMS with minor modifications.

There were two Class 3 locomotive types; a 2-6-2 tank engine and a 2-6-0 tender version of it, which were intended to meet a need for engines midway in power and axle load between the Class 4 2-6-4Ts and 4-6-0s on the one hand, and the Class 2s on the other. They had the Swindon No 4 boiler, but modified with greater superheat and a dome. The LMS Class 2 2-6-0 and 2-6-2 tank engine, with their light 13 ton axle loading, were included, but with minor modifications. All these engines had rocking grates, self-cleaning smokeboxes, and self-emptying ashpans. Copper fireboxes were used, because, owing to the variation in the quality of water available, they gave better service than steel. The well-tried and reliable Walschaerts valve gear was selected. Draughting had been the subject of tests at Rugby and Swindon, and the system adopted was based on the findings of these tests. It had been shown that double, and certain other special, blastpipe arrangements could give improved results at maximum outputs, but were inferior in performance at lower outputs, and that through the whole range they were less satisfactory than the single blastpipe. Because the majority of locomotive work demands less than the maximum output, the single blastpipe and chimney were retained for most of these engines. Steam passages, however, were designed in accordance with the principles established by Monsieur André Chapelon.

In October 1952 there was a bad smash at Harrow in which LMS Pacific No 46202, rebuilt from the turbine locomotive, was completely wrecked. This gave Riddles the opportunity to obtain authority to build a new Class 8 Pacific with which running experience might be gained for the design of future Class 8 engines. This prototype locomotive was the three-cylinder No 71000 *Duke of Gloucester*, with Caprotti valve gear, a double chimney, and the same boiler as the Class 7 Pacifics, but with a larger grate.

The last of the 12 types was the heavy freight engine. The Chief Draughtsmen's Committee had proposed a 2-8-2. This Riddles disliked because such a wheel arrangement entailed some loss of adhesion, and he believed that little would be gained in power over existing 2-8-0s. In the light of experience with his previous very successful Austerity 10-coupled freight engine, he said that he wanted a 2-10-0, but would like confirmation that 5ft coupled wheels could be used with a wide firebox. Investigation showed this to be possible and the 2-10-0 was built. In the event these Class 9 2-10-0s were perhaps the most successful heavy freight steam locomotives ever to run in the British Isles. Apart from their ability as freight engines, they soon showed that they could run very freely at high speeds, and there were well documented reports of their exceeding 90 mile/h.

These 12 classes, incorporating all the best practices of the past, met the needs of the time for simple, free-steaming engines, which were easy to maintain and able to handle without difficulty the traffic of the railway. There was only one Class 8 Pacific, however, and this was still on trials when steam construction came to an end. Of the others, Riddles believes that his Class 6

Pacific was a mistake, and that had he made it a 4-8-0 the extra adhesion would have provided a solution to traffic problems in Scotland.

Much has already been written about the design and performances of the Riddles locomotives, and it is not proposed to do so again here. Few could have anticipated, however, that their existence would be so brief; but it is perhaps a tribute to their general excellence that many of the diesel locomotives which were to have replaced them, went to the breaker's yard, while some of the steam types were still running.

Riddles' conviction that electric traction was the motive power of the future has already been mentioned. His interest in it had been first aroused when, as an apprentice at Crewe, he had read an article in which it was stated that through electrification the capacity of a line could be increased by 30%. This so impressed him that he attended classes in practical electrical engineering. The opportunity to take practical steps towards electrification came in March 1951 when the French Railways (SNCF) invited him to attend a demonstration at Annécy of the 25kV 50Hz ac system that they had erected on the 55-mile stretch of track between Aix-le-Bains and Laroche-sur-Foron on the Geneva-Chamonix line. Riddles took with him S.B. Warder, who had succeeded Cock as his Chief Electrical Engineer. Also present were representatives of many British firms. Riddles was so impressed with the demonstration, and with the whole concept of 50Hz traction, that he invited the representatives of the British firms to a cocktail party and discussed with them the possibilities of introducing the system into Great Britain. It so happened that a few weeks earlier the Railway Executive had decided to abandon the 6,600V 25Hz ac electrified system on the nine-mile line between Morecambe and Heysham and replace it by push-pull steam operation, because the equipment, installed by the

Midland Railway in 1908, was worn out. Remembering this, Riddles said to his guests that if they would go back and persuade their principals to supply the equipment free, he would ask the Railway Executive to reverse their decision and would provide the vehicles and facilities to try out 50Hz traction on the Morecambe and Heysham line. The representatives agreed, as did their firms, and the work of electrifying the line under the new system was carried out, under the direction of Warder, as a joint experiment in association with the British Electricity Authority, the English Electric Company, and British Insulated Callenders Cables. The old voltage of 6,600 was retained temporarily but the new equipment was designed for 20kV. Riddles provided three ex-LNWR three-coach electric train sets which had been built in 1914 and which had been made surplus by the closing to passenger traffic in 1940 of the Willesden-Earls Court line. These coaches were converted at Wolverton for their new role, and each set comprised a motor coach, a trailer, and a driving trailer. The first trains were being run in November 1952, within one year of starting the project, and full public service began on 17 August 1953. (It was Warder who was subsequently responsible for the electrification on the 50Hz ac system of the whole of the old LNWR main line from Euston to Liverpool and Manchester, and he was awarded the Gold Medal of the Institution of Locomotive Engineers for his work on electrification – a very rare distinction.)

Note

Nearly all the information contained in this chapter was supplied to me by Mr R. A. Riddles.

Below: Diagram of 2-8-2.

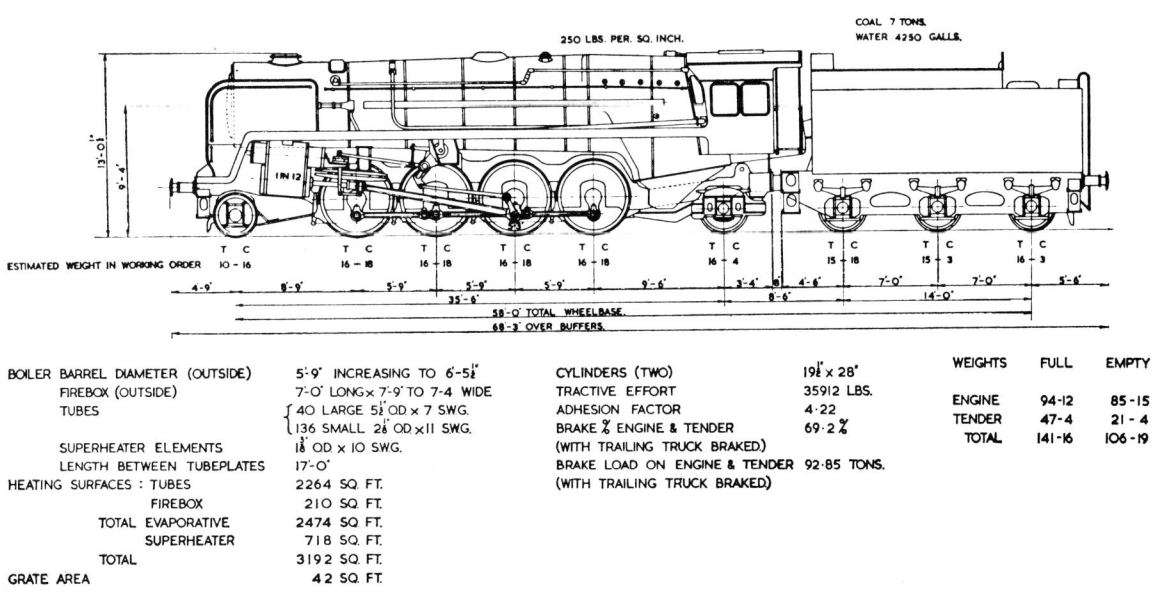

BOILER BARREL DIAMETER (OUTSIDE)	5'-9" INCREASING TO 6'-5¼"	
FIREBOX (OUTSIDE)	7'-0" LONG × 7'-9" TO 7-4 WIDE	
TUBES	40 LARGE 5⅛" OD × 7 SWG.	
	136 SMALL 2⅛" OD × 11 SWG.	
SUPERHEATER ELEMENTS	1⅛" OD × 10 SWG.	
LENGTH BETWEEN TUBEPLATES	17'-0"	
HEATING SURFACES : TUBES	2264 SQ. FT.	
FIREBOX	210 SQ. FT.	
TOTAL EVAPORATIVE	2474 SQ. FT.	
SUPERHEATER	718 SQ. FT.	
TOTAL	3192 SQ. FT.	
GRATE AREA	42 SQ. FT.	

CYLINDERS (TWO)	19¼" × 28"
TRACTIVE EFFORT	35912 LBS.
ADHESION FACTOR	4·22
BRAKE % ENGINE & TENDER	69·2 %
(WITH TRAILING TRUCK BRAKED)	
BRAKE LOAD ON ENGINE & TENDER	92·85 TONS.
(WITH TRAILING TRUCK BRAKED)	

WEIGHTS	FULL	EMPTY
ENGINE	94-12	85-15
TENDER	47-4	21-4
TOTAL	141-16	106-19

PROPOSED CLASS 8 2-8-2 ENGINE.

Above left: J. F. Harrison

Above: R. C. Bond

Left: R.A. Riddles

Above right: Early 1948 saw the first signs of a return to normality, although the initiatives were largely due to the Big Four. 'Duchess' 4-6-2 No 6230 *Duchess of Buccleuch* passes Berkhamsted with the down 'Royal Scot' on 25 March 1948. The train had been reintroduced as a named train the previous month./*H.C. Casserley*

Right: The Eastern Region had returned the 'Flying Scotsman' as a non-stop working from 31 May 1948. Here A4 4-6-2 No 60012 *Commonwealth of Australia* passes Newcastle without stopping on 28 July 1948. /*Kenneth C. Foster*

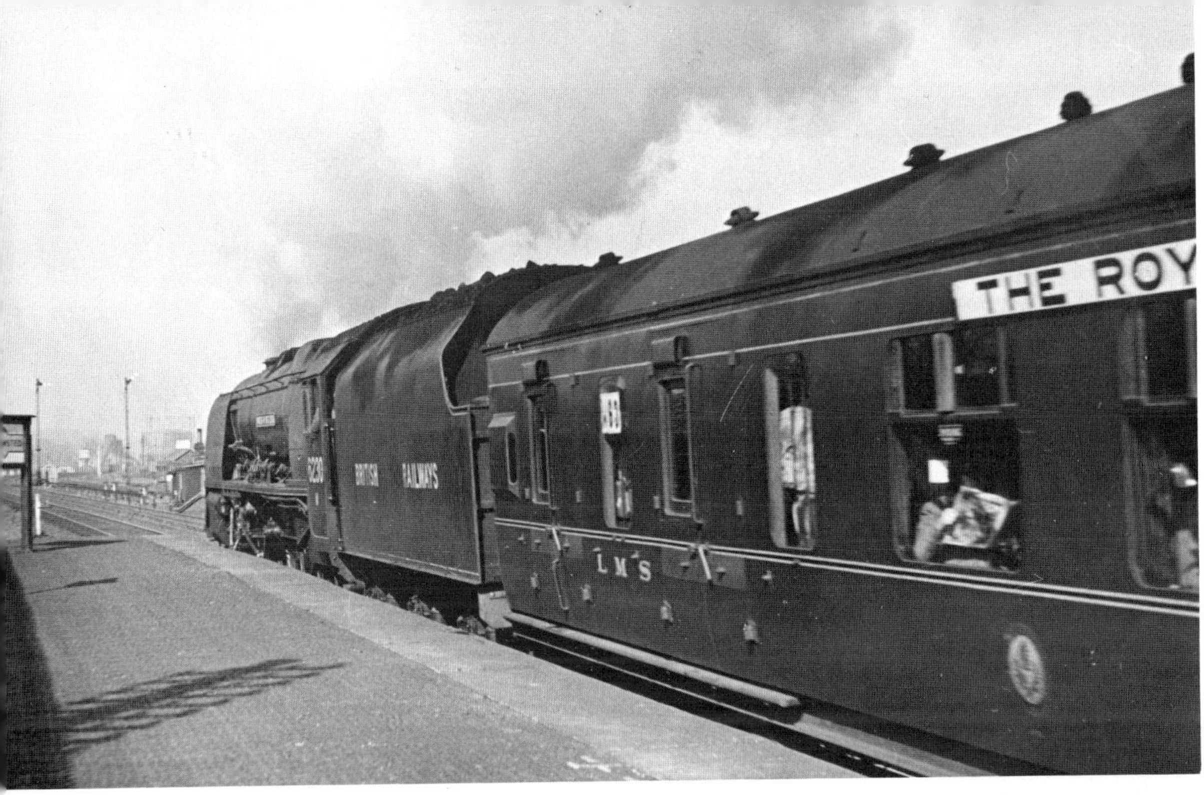
THE ROY
BRITISH RAILWAYS
LMS

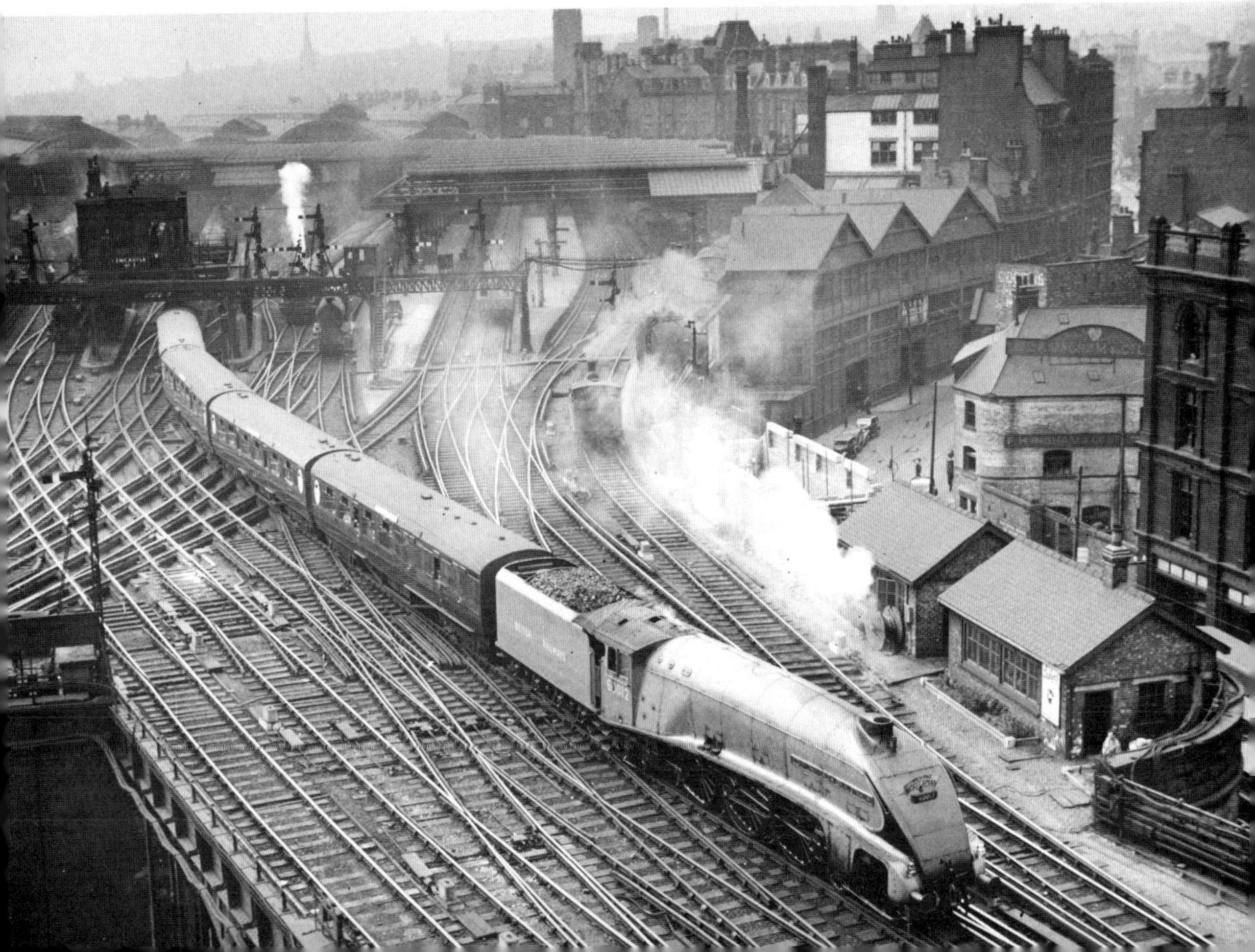

Left: Early priority was given to renumbering. A 'Royal Scot' becomes No 46124 at Crewe early in 1948./*BR*

Below: The SR offered the most experience with electric traction. Early in 1949 a down Portsmouth fast passes Clapham Junction. /*C.C.B. Herbert*

Above right: Some valuable data was available on the economics of diesel shunters, even if nothing was to hand on main line locomotives. /*BR*

Centre right: The Locomotive Exchanges of 1948 were an attempt to assess the strengths, or weaknesses, of 'Big Four' designs. Ex-LMS rebuilt 'Royal Scot' 4-6-0 No 46162 *Royal Westminster Rifleman* arrives at Kings Cross with a Leeds express on 30 April 1948, the dynamometer car next to its tender. Waiting to leave the terminus is A3 No 59 *Tracery*. /*C.C.B. Herbert*

Below right: Progress continued with existing designs. A 'West Country' takes shape in Brighton Works in the late 1940s./*C.R.L. Coles*

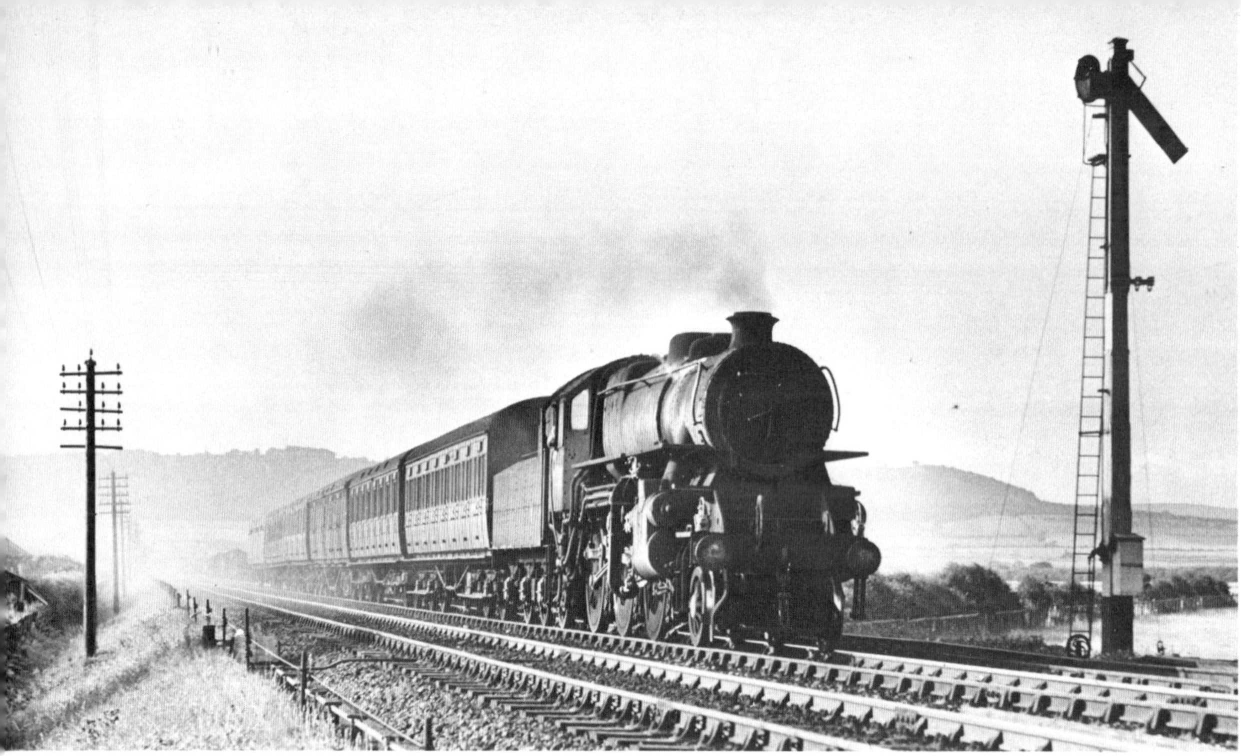

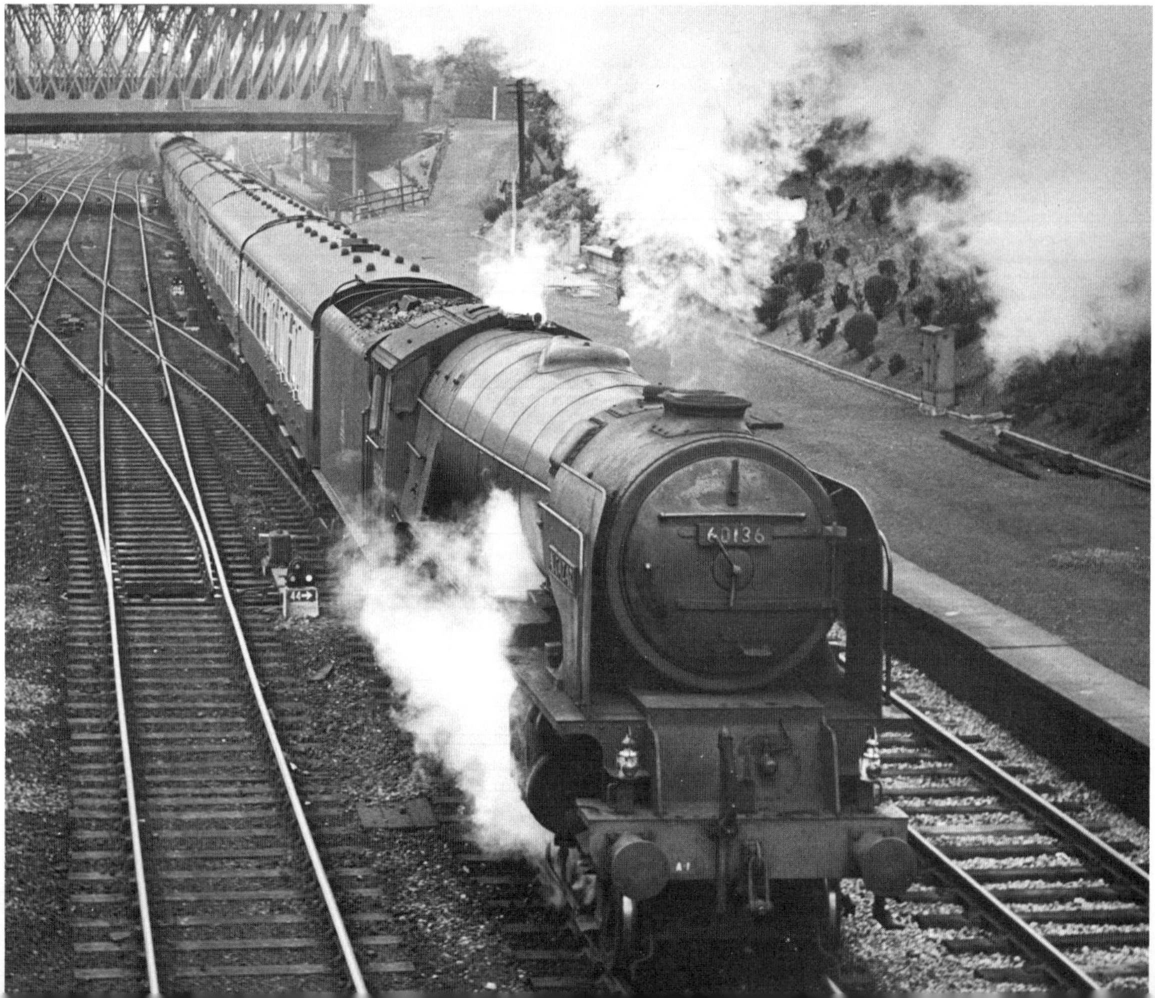
60136
44→

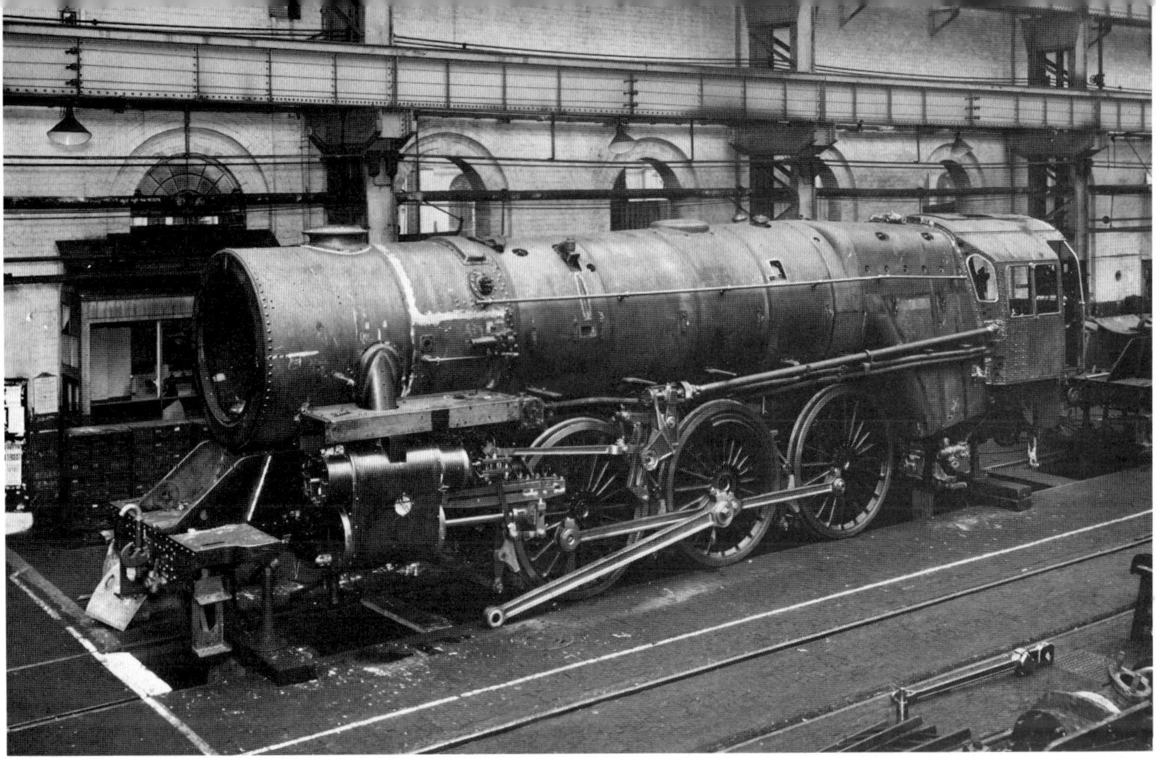

Top left: An example of a new locomotive of a regional design working on a 'foreign' territory: LMS design Class 4 2-6-0 No 43050 approaches Redcar East, NER, with the 08.00 express to Middlesbrough and Darlington on 15 August 1951./*P.H. Wells*

Left: The ER's principal express passenger motive power demands were met by the construction of Class A1 4-6-2s, such as No 60136 *Alcazar* leaving York on a Glasgow-Kings Cross express in the early 1950s. /*Eric Treacy*

Top: Pride of place in the BR Standard designs went to the 'Britannia' Pacifics. Here *Britannia* is under construction in Crewe Works erecting shop in January 1951./*BR*

Above: The finished result: *Britannia,* No 70000, works hard near Manor Park with down 'The Norfolkman' of 26 February 1951. /*R.E. Vincent*

Right: One of the best of the BR Standards: down empties rumble through Oakley cutting, on the Midland main line, behind a 9F 2-10-0 in 1959./*H.C. Prudden*

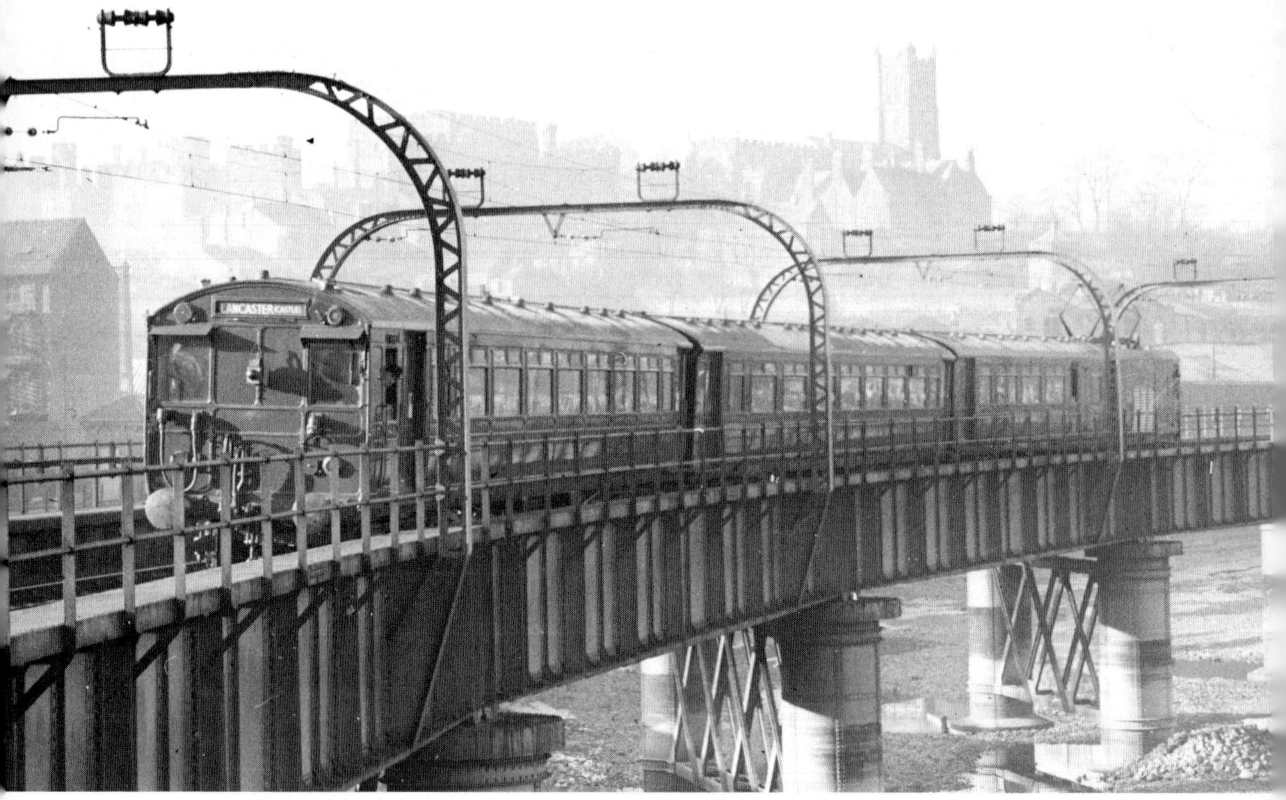

Top: BR Standard line-up. The IRC Exhibition at Willesden in 1955
featuring (left to right) a Class 9F, *Duke of Gloucester,* a Class 4 2-6-4T,
a 'Britannia', a Class 5 4-6-0 and a Class 3 2-6-0.

Above: The real promise lay with 50Hz electrification and Riddles'
foresight lay in the decision to use the Lancaster-Morecambe-Heysham
line as a test-bed. The first run of an emu of 11 November 1952 with the
converted LNWR stock crossing the River Lune bridge, Lancaster.
/C.C.B. Herbert

2
Diesel Inception

In 1932 the London & North Eastern Railway tested a diesel-electric railcar in the Newcastle area. It had been built by Armstrong Whitworth & Company and the tests were satisfactory enough for two more to be ordered. In 1934 all three were taken into operating stock and named, respectively, *Tyneside Venturer, Lady Hamilton,* and *Northumbrian.*[1] The Great Western followed, but on a much larger scale, with diesel-mechanical railcars. The first one, built by the Associated Equipment Company of Southall (AEC), went into service on 4 December 1933, operating in the Reading area on local journeys. It had a single diesel engine of 121hp and a streamlined body. Three more were constructed, but these were intended for express services, with a maximum speed of 75-80 mile/h and driven by two of the 121hp engines, one for each bogie. These AEC engines and their transmissions were similar to those used on the London buses. A buffet section was included on each of the express cars, which were used on a Cardiff-Birmingham service from 1934 till about 1940. After the war they ran between Swansea, Newport, and Cheltenham. A total of 38 diesel cars were eventually built, the last in February 1942; the final four forming two twin units to take over the Birmingham-Cardiff service from the original express cars. Later a standard carriage was introduced between the two power cars to form a three-car train, with a buffet counter and lavatories. Other services operated by the Great Western diesel cars included business trains between Oxford and Hereford; Bristol and Cardiff; and Bristol and Weymouth, as well as branch and subsidiary trains with railcars geared down to a maximum speed of 40 mile/h to enable them to haul two standard carriages.[2]

But if the Great Western could perhaps claim to be the first to operate diesel traction in regular service on a considerable scale, it was the London Midland & Scottish Railway which really took the lead in diesel development. Indeed, in 1928, four years before the LNER purchase, the LMS tested a diesel-electric four-car train, with a Beardmore 500hp engine, between Blackpool and Lytham; but the train was not a success, and nothing came of it.

LMS interest was first really aroused during the depression of 1931 by the prospect of the economies that could be realised with diesel shunters operated by one man. In the years 1932-34 11 such shunters were ordered, nine with a mechanical transmission and two with electric. In view of future policy, it is of interest that one of these latter, built by Armstrong Whitworth, had a Sulzer engine, and the other was English Electric built and powered. In the purchase of these various shunters, the LMS adopted a policy (later followed by British

Railways) of trying everything available before deciding on a standard type. However, from English Electric came C. E. Fairburn as Electrical Engineer of the LMS. He would only consider electric transmission, and so the diesel-electric shunter was selected for future development, with an engine of 300-350hp, which experience showed was the most suitable. In 1935 20 further diesel-electric shunters were ordered, of which 10 came from English Electric and 10 from Armstrong Whitworth. The former were the more satisfactory and 40 more were ordered, with the design modified to include a jackshaft drive. These were delivered in 1939. In a subsequent order the jackshaft drive was dispensed with and there were two nose-suspended motors driving the outer coupled axles direct through double reduction gearing. Twenty of these went into service in 1944, and the last six were of the design that became standard for the LMS and for British Railways.[3] The diesel-electric shunter proved so successful that the LMS decided to build no more steam shunting engines.

On the Southern Railway, in 1936, R.E.L. Maunsell, the Chief Mechanical Engineer, obtained authority to purchase three six-coupled diesel-electric shunters for comparative trials with the Class Z 0-8-0 tank engines. The mechanical parts were constructed at Ashford, and English Electric supplied the power units. The maximum output was 350hp at 680rev/min. All three were employed in the yards at Norwood and they replaced four steam shunting engines. Three years later O.V.S. Bulleid was authorised to build eight more diesel-electric shunters at Eastleigh; but the outbreak of war delayed construction, and it was not till April 1949 that delivery started – though from Ashford. They were very similar in many details to the prewar LMS design.[4]

On the London & North Eastern Railway there were plans in 1947 to purchase 176 diesel-electric shunters of 350hp to replace 217 steam shunting engines.[5]

The first Great Western diesel-electric shunting locomotives, of 360hp, were built by R. & W. Hawthorn, Leslie, & Company, in April 1936; English Electric again supplying the power units. In 1948 six more very similar shunters were built at Swindon; though the following year Swindon built one with a Brush two-stroke engine and Brush electrical gear.[6]

At the end of 1942 Sir William Stanier was seconded to the Ministry of Production and Fairburn was appointed Acting CME. At the end of 1944 Stanier resigned from the LMS and early in 1945 Fairburn was appointed in his place. H. G. Ivatt, who had been Principal Assistant to Stanier for Locomotives, remained in the same appointment with Fairburn. Ivatt had served in the Royal Army

Service Corps during World War I and had then become extremely interested in internal combustion engines. Following the success of the diesel shunters, Ivatt became fascinated with the idea of building a diesel-electric passenger locomotive. He suggested this to Fairburn in 1945, but without much success. In October that year, however, Fairburn died suddenly, and Ivatt, after succeeding him in an acting capacity, became CME in January 1946. He now saw possibilities of getting his diesel express locomotive, and mentioned it to Sir William Wood, President of the LMS. A few days after this Riddles was appointed Vice President for Engineering, and got authority from the Board for the construction of a twin-unit express locomotive and also a single locomotive for secondary services. A very large sum of money was entailed, but even so, Ivatt's estimate for the express locomotives was far below the actual cost, and Riddles had to ask for more money long before the first of the two was completed.[7]

Ivatt chose English Electric to provide the power equipment for his express engines, which were to be built at Derby; the Chief Draughtsman, T. F. Coleman, and his staff being responsible for the design of the mechanical parts. English Electric, at the time, were the obvious choice, for the company had more experience than other British firms in diesel traction, and was at that time engaged in building 12 1,600hp main line locomotives for Egypt. Ivatt chose this same engine for the LMS locomotives. The North British Locomotive Company was given the main contract for the secondary services locomotive, for which Davey Paxman & Company supplied the engines and British Thomson-Houston the electrical equipment.[8]

The first of the twin express locomotives, No 10000, was driven proudly by Ivatt out of the Derby shops on 8 December 1947. Ivatt had had the floor plates made with the letters LMS cast in, and the same letters appeared raised in silver on the black sides, so that, with Nationalisation due in a few days, there could be no doubt as to the original ownership. On 16 December No 10000 ran to Euston for official inspection, along with the new Pacific No 6256 *Sir William A. Stanier, FRS*. It then returned to Derby for outstanding work to be completed, and this, it must be admitted, was not finished until after Nationalisation. No 10001, the sister engine, appeared from Derby in July 1948, but without, of course, the LMS initials.[9] In 1951 No 10000 lost them from the cab sides, but Ivatt had seen to it that those on the floor plates were irremovable!

On 1 June 1949 there was an inaugural run of the two locomotives, hauling the 'Royal Scot' from Euston to Glasgow, and the London Midland Region of British Railways produced a nicely illustrated brochure to commemorate the event. The following particulars were given in respect of each of these Co-Co type locomotives: engine, English Electric Type 16SVT 16-cylinder, four-stroke vee with turbo-superchargers, giving 1,600hp at 750rev/min, and with cylinders of 10in bore and 12in stroke; generator, English Electric type 823A, supplying six traction motors of English Electric type 519/1B;

tractive effort 41,400lb; weight in working order 127 tons 13cwt; and maximum speed 93mile/h.

Small gangway doors were provided at each end of both locomotives, so that they could be coupled together in any order, enabling the fireman to pass from one end to the other whilst the train was in motion. For the inaugural trip a special adaptor gangway had been fitted so that visits could be made from the train by official guests. A description of what the visitor would see on his passage through the locomotives was included in the brochure, and is included here because of its special interest in relation to the first British main line diesel locomotives.

'On entering the locomotive from the train via the special gangway, the machine on the left is the traction motor blower which blows cooling air into the main traction motors on the adjacent bogie. This runs continuously. The machine on the right is the air compressor which provides compressed air for the electrical equipment, horn, road wheel sanding, windscreen washing, windscreen wipers and also a supply of air for fuelling purposes. Next is the cab. Notice also the headlight switches and cab heater switches. The de-mister switches provide hot air through the ducts at the bottom of the cab windows to assist in keeping the screens clean. Notice the boiling ring for the driver's tea.

'After passing the main fuel tank, notice the two motor driven vacuum exhausters, one each side of the radiator arch, and the cooling fan motor overhead. Passing the diesel engine notice the four turbo-superchargers, one on each corner of the engine at about head height. These provide compressed air for the engine air intake. The turbine wheel is driven by exhaust gas from the engine and runs at some 23,000 revolutions per minute on full load. Not only does this machine increase the available output from the diesel engine by some 30 to 40%, but also acts as a silencer for the exhaust gases. The engine has three operating speeds, 425rpm, 600rpm, and 750rpm, dependent upon the power demands by the driver. Passing the flywheel and of the engine notice the warm air exhaled by the cooling fan on the main generator.

'Passing through the bulkhead door separating the engine compartment from the generator compartment, notice the rows of air filters set low down on the body sides; this compartment is generally referred to as the clean air compartment, since all the air going in passes through these filters before it is drawn through the main generator for cooling purposes. The difference in temperature between this compartment and the engine compartment is marked, particularly on a cold day. The control cabinet is also installed in this compartment, and it is very necessary that conditions should be as free from dust as possible. On top of the control cabinet are various meters for use by maintenance staff and other technical staff who may travel from time to time. The doors to the clean air compartment are spring loaded into a closed position and provided with a rubber gasket for sealing purposes.

'Passing through the clean air compartment next comes the equipment devoted to carriage warming; the principal item of course is the carriage warming boiler, an oil fired fully automatic boiler producing 1,000lb of steam per hour, solely for the purpose of heating the train. It is part of the fireman's duty to light the boiler, but normally no further attention is required. The circular tanks mounted above the boiler water tanks are reservoirs for compressed air. A curious crackling metallic noise occurs when the compressors are running and is probably caused by a combination of the valve gear on the compressors, and the cooling pipe work from the compressors to these cylinders. It is not necessary to do more than indicate the toilet tucked away in a corner. Leading from this compartment is the second cab which is slightly different in that it contains the generator field resistances but no boiling ring.

'Passing through the nose and the corridor connection to the next unit, notice that this unit is running in reverse as compared to the preceding unit.

'The locomotives are fitted with a comprehensive built in CO_2 fire fighting equipment with nozzles at strategic points. Operation is by remote control from the driving cabs. Portable CO_2 equipment is also provided.

'Finally, after to what to the uninitiated must seem a lengthy, noisy and somewhat tortuous journey, comes the driver's cab.'

As a description of a diesel-electric locomotive, this could hardly be bettered, for in clear and simple language it explains to the layman the main components of the machine and how they work.

The brochure also gives the current thinking as to how the diesel locomotive compared with its steam predecessor. The steam locomotive was simple in construction and operation, was cheap to build and maintain, was mechanically very reliable, was flexible in operation, and burned home-produced fuel. On the other hand, the diesel had an even torque resulting in a lower factor of adhesion and a higher starting effort for the same weight on the coupled wheels. It was believed at this time that there was no hammer blow and that therefore it could have a higher axle loading. It was ready for service at any time, and one train crew could control more than one unit. There was no smoke to obscure vision or rot structures, no stops for coal or water, and no ash to dispose of or fire to clean; it was thus available for a large proportion of its time in service. Furthermore, its fuel oil was easy to handle and to transport in bulk. Its thermal efficiency was higher than that of the steam engine and it provided better conditions for the footplate staff.

The final arbiter between the two different forms of motive power was the cost. Whilst the diesel locomotive consumed much less fuel by weight than the steam locomotive, and had a higher thermal efficiency, the cost of the fuel it consumed was so much more expensive that it was considered at this time that the cost per mile of the two types of traction was about equal. But in the United Kingdom at that time the first cost of a diesel locomotive was about four times greater than that of a steam locomotive of comparable power. Against this, the diesel, because of its greater availability, should be able to replace more than one steam engine. It was thought, however (wrongly, as it transpired) that to take advantage

of this a very high annual mileage was necessary; a difficulty that did not arise in America, but in the United Kingdom high annual mileages are difficult to achieve.

In 1949, then, there was nothing to make the average locomotive engineer wish to change from the well-tried and reliable steam locomotive to the newer power unless, and until, its advantages were proved by very extensive trials.

Nos 10000 and 10001 were in fact, says R. C. Bond,[10] very good engines and superior to their near contemporaries on the Southern Region. These latter locomotives were ordered for the Southern Railway, but the first, No 10201, was not ready until November 1950. O. V. S. Bulleid, CME of the Southern Railway, was responsible for the mechanical design, and C. M. Cock, the Chief Electrical Engineer of the SR (and later, of course, Riddles' Electrical Engineer on British Railways) was responsible for the electrical part. The power equipment was supplied by English Electric and the diesel engine was the same as that used in the two LMS locomotives. The Southern had decided on three locomotives, but the third was deferred until experience had been obtained with the first two. Construction started at Ashford in 1949. The locomotive weight of 135 tons was, however, too much for two six-wheeled bogies, as on the LMS, for the axle load would have been unacceptably great. Two-wheeled pony trucks were therefore added at the outer ends of each bogie to spread the load. The second locomotive, No 10202, was completed in September 1951.

There were now four diesel-electric express locomotives available for trials, but Riddles says that it was difficult to get them properly tested because the operating people disliked them, and either could not or would not find suitable paths which would permit of their maximum use. Part of the operating objection was that they did not fit in with the 'link' system. Top link drivers shared the top jobs in rotation, which meant that, with the diesels being used on the most important expresses, they might drive a diesel one day and then exclusively steam engines for the next week or so. But unless all of them were thoroughly trained in diesel operation, much trouble could result. For instance, there was an occasion when, hauling the 'Night Scot', the two LMS diesels stuck on the Camden bank. A relief driver was sent for, and the fireman of this, being interested in diesels, climbed in and asked what the trouble was. 'B . . . if I know', replied the driver. The fireman looked round, pushed the overload release button, and said, 'Now start', and it did. The diesels had been worked too hard up the bank![11]

It was clear to Riddles that the diesels were not getting the best usage, and he accordingly arranged that the four should be allocated to the Southern Region, where, having a much smaller proportion of steam locomotives, they were anxious to try the new power. The Southern diagrammed the diesels so that a maximum mileage could be obtained from them every day. On the whole the results were satisfactory, though there were a number of teething troubles.[12]

Ivatt, says Riddles, was undoubtedly the pioneer in main line diesel locomotives. After his retirement from the railway he became consultant to the Brush company, and it was largely his knowledge that was responsible for Brush's early success.[13]

The 800hp secondary services locomotive was completed in May 1950 with a Paxman 827hp engine. It carried out trials on secondary passenger duties from Willesden and Rugby. Another and much more unconventional diesel locomotive which was tried out on the Midland main line was that designed by Col. L. F. R. Fell, a Rolls-Royce engineer. It was equipped with an ingenious mechanical drive and a 4-8-4 wheel arrangement. Fell persuaded Ivatt to give his system a trial. The locomotive did good work for a period but spent too much time out of service under repair.[14]

The LNER had apparently formulated tentative plans to convert the East Coast Anglo-Scottish services to diesel traction, with 25 diesels replacing 32 Pacifics, and Hurcomb expressed disappointment that the Railway Executive had apparently decided not to go ahead with the scheme.[15] However, J. F. Harrison says that he knew that the LNE Board had discussed such a plan, but never heard that they had decided on it. He does not think that Peppercorn would have been in favour, as so much could be done by his A1 Pacifics, without having to arrange new maintenance facilities, training, etc.[16] It certainly seems unlikely that the LNE Board would have come to such a decision without informing the CME.

The Great Western's approach to possible future main line motive power differed, as one would expect of this very individualistic concern, from that of any other railway. In 1946 the Company ordered two gas turbine-electric locomotives, one from the Swiss firm of Brown-Boveri and the other from Metropolitan-Vickers. The Brown-Boveri locomotive was based on one which had been in service in Switzerland since 1941. It was delivered in 1950 and, after trials, went into service as No 18000, working express trains between Paddington and Plymouth and between Paddington and Bristol. It was restricted to the same routes as the 'King' class 4-6-0s. The wheel arrangement was A1A-A1A, and the 2,500hp turbine drove a generator supplying current to four traction motors. The Metropolitan-Vickers locomotive, No 18100, arrived in December 1951. It had a 3,000hp gas turbine and a Co-Co wheel arrangement. Results were disappointing because both designs were found to consume nearly as much fuel when idling, or running under reduced power, as they did under full load. They did not compare, therefore, with diesel locomotives and they had short lives. No 18000 ran intermittently for 10 years and was withdrawn in December 1960; while No 18100 was withdrawn in 1958 and converted into an experimental 25kV electric locomotive for crew training.[17]

The Committee on Motive Power delivered its report to the Railway Executive in 1951. It referred to the great success of diesel traction in America and of electrification and diesel railcars in Europe. It remarked, more debatably, that these forms of traction had made possible a vast improvement in the speed and character of passenger traffic and in the operation of freight traffic, and an improvement in the working conditions of the staff. It concluded that, while further improvements could be made to steam locomotives, there were no fundamental design changes by which the inherent limitations of steam traction could be overcome; and that further substantial improvements in the standards of service would involve increasing reliance on electrical or diesel traction. (This latter was an erroneous deduction because obviously the standards of service could be restored to the vastly higher standards prevailing with steam before the war.)

The report recommended that the Great Northern Railway route from Kings Cross to Grantham should be electrified; that there should be a large scale trial of diesel traction on main line services, using 2,000hp locomotives; that diesel railcars should replace steam on a wide range of cross-country and other secondary services; and that the number of diesel shunters should be greatly increased.

The last recommendation was unnecessary because the Railway Executive was already engaged on a five-year plan of building diesel shunting locomotives. Main line electrification was of course accepted in principle, though not necessarily giving priority to the route recommended. As regards main line tests of diesel traction, there were as yet no 2,000hp single-unit locomotives, but one was in hand for the Southern Region, and the large scale tests of this power, the Committee suggested, should await the satisfactory outcome of its trials. In the event of their being successful, 100 2,000hp locomotives should be ordered for trial running, together with a number of smaller units for branch line and secondary duties. In the meantime the limited experiments with the four existing diesel express units should be continued.

The Railway Executive rejected that part of the report dealing with the main line trials. They could see no reason in spending £7 million on 100 2,000hp locomotives when the 1,600hp locomotives already in service were costing more to operate relatively high mileage rosters than steam Pacifics, even when working as single units. In addition, 1,600hp locomotives were capable of working most of the traffic on British Railways, so that they believed that those already in service were sufficient to enable a reliable assessment to be made as to whether or not main line diesel traction would be financially justified. On the other hand, the recommendation for diesel operation on secondary services was accepted, and a working party was set up to consider the scope of lightweight diesel trains. In March 1952 it presented a report recommending areas that were considered suitable for the operation of such trains. This was accepted and plans to implement it were put in hand.[18] There was fortunately a pattern to follow, for in that same year the Ulster Transport Authority, at the instigation of its Chairman, F. Pope, had put into service railcars equipped with underfloor-mounted horizontal diesel engines with hydraulic transmission. Pope was now a member of the British Transport Commission, and in 1954 very similar units appeared on British Railways.[19]

It was not till March 1954 that the Southern 2,000hp diesel-electric locomotive, No 10203, was completed at Brighton, with the English Electric 16SVT engine Mark II, giving 2,000hp at 850rev/min. With the arrival of this locomotive on British Railways, the first stage of the transition from steam to diesel may be said to have ended.

Notes

1 Brown, F. A. S.; *Nigel Gresley: Locomotive Engineer;* Ian Allan Ltd, 1961, pp131-2
2 Doherty, J. M.; *Diesel Locomotive Practice;* Odhams Press, 1962, pp 54-5, *The Locomotives of the Great Western Railway,* Parts 11 and 12; Railway Correspondence & Travel Society, 1956 & 1974.
3 Riddles, R. A.; Information to the Author
4 Bradley, D. L.; *Locomotives of the Southern Railway;* Railway Correspondence & Travel Society, 1975
5 *The Locomotives of the L.N.E.R., Part 1;* Railway Correspondence & Travel Society, 1963
6 *The Locomotives of the Great Western Railway,* op cit
7 Riddles, R. A.; op cit
8 Cox, E. S.; *Locomotive Panorama, Vol 1;* Ian Allan Ltd, 1965, pp155-8
9 Riddles, op cit
10 Bond, R.C.; Information to the Author
11 Riddles, op cit
12 ibid
13 ibid
14 Bond, Roland C.; *A Lifetime with Locomotives;* Cambridge, Goose & Sons, 1975, p239
15 ibid, p213
16 J. F. Harrison, information to the Author
17 *The Locomotives of the Great Western Railway,* op cit
18 Bond, op cit, pp213f
19 Doherty, op cit, Bond, op cit, p239

Above: End of the LMS and a significant encounter. Euston station on 16 December 1947 with Pacific No 6256 *Sir William A. Stanier FRS* (left) and No 10000./*BR*

Right. The earliest days of GWR railcars. No 1 poses with a 'King' and a 'Duke' early in 1934. /*Ian Allan Library*

Left: 'Big Four' diesel shunter. The Southern's No 3 diesel-electric shunter is in for repair at Norwood Junction shed on 28 April 1948. /*N.F. Parker*

Below: Diesel-electric shunter production by the LMS at Derby Works in 1947/*BR*

Right: The LMS's No 10000 under construction at Derby in 1947./*BR*

Below right: New dawn: Nos 10001 and 10000 at Carlisle on the up 'Royal Scot'./*Eric Treacy*

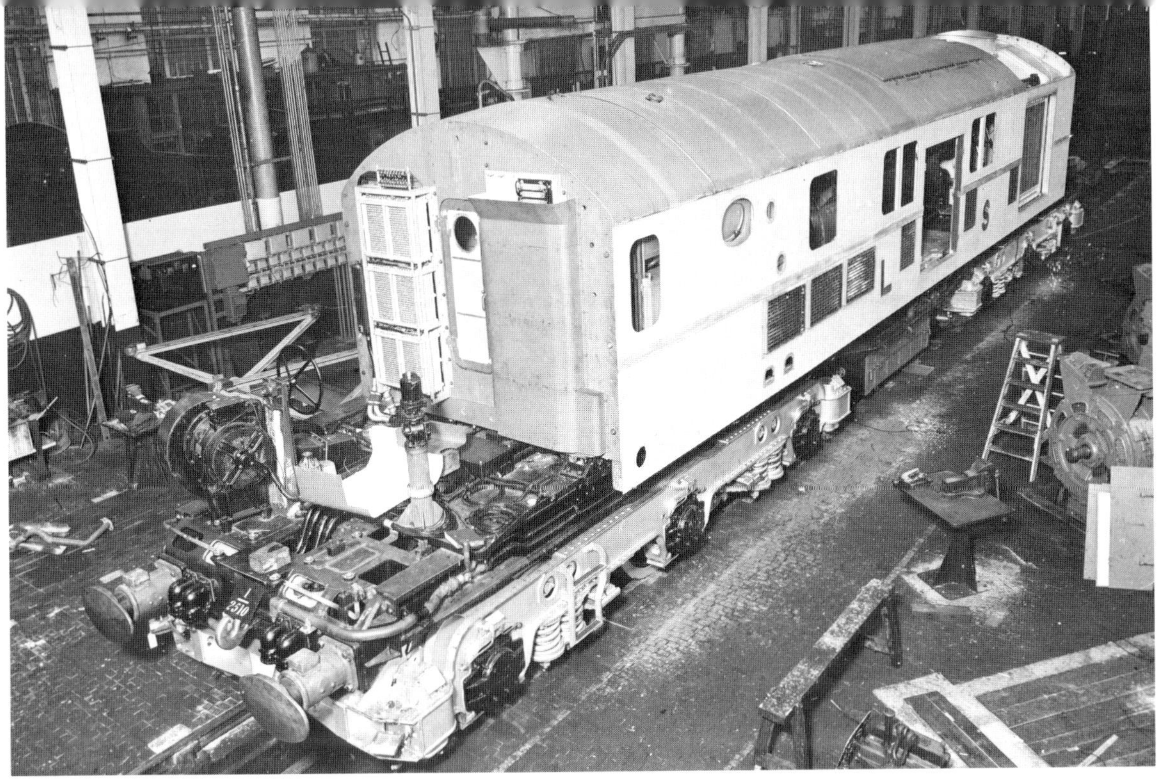

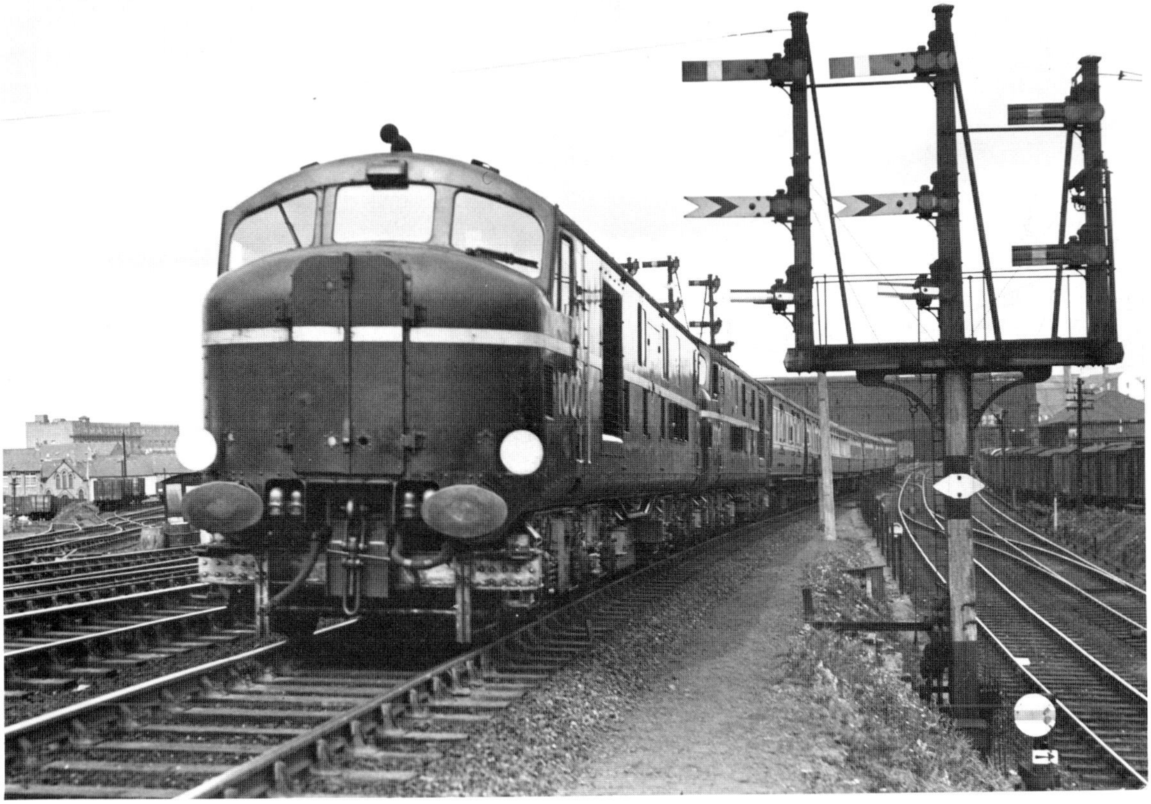

Left: No 10000 on the SR, seen leaving Southampton Central on the 08.30 Waterloo-Bournemouth on 7 March 1953.

Below left: Last of the Southern main line diesels, No 10203, on test with Swindon's dynamometer car in July 1955 at Andover. /*G. Wheeler*

Right: The secondary services 800hp Bo-Bo, No 10800, with BTH electrical equipment and Paxman engine, seen here on trial on the SR. /*GEC*

Below: Col Fell's mechanical drive 4-8-4 main line diesel No 10100, near Kibworth with a St Pancras-bound express in July 1952, rubbing shoulders with an ex-MR 0-6-0. /*E.D. Bruton*

Bottom: The Great Western's Brown Boveri gas turbine locomotive No 18000, near Corsham with the up 12.00 Bristol-Paddington in May 1951. /*G.J. Jefferson*

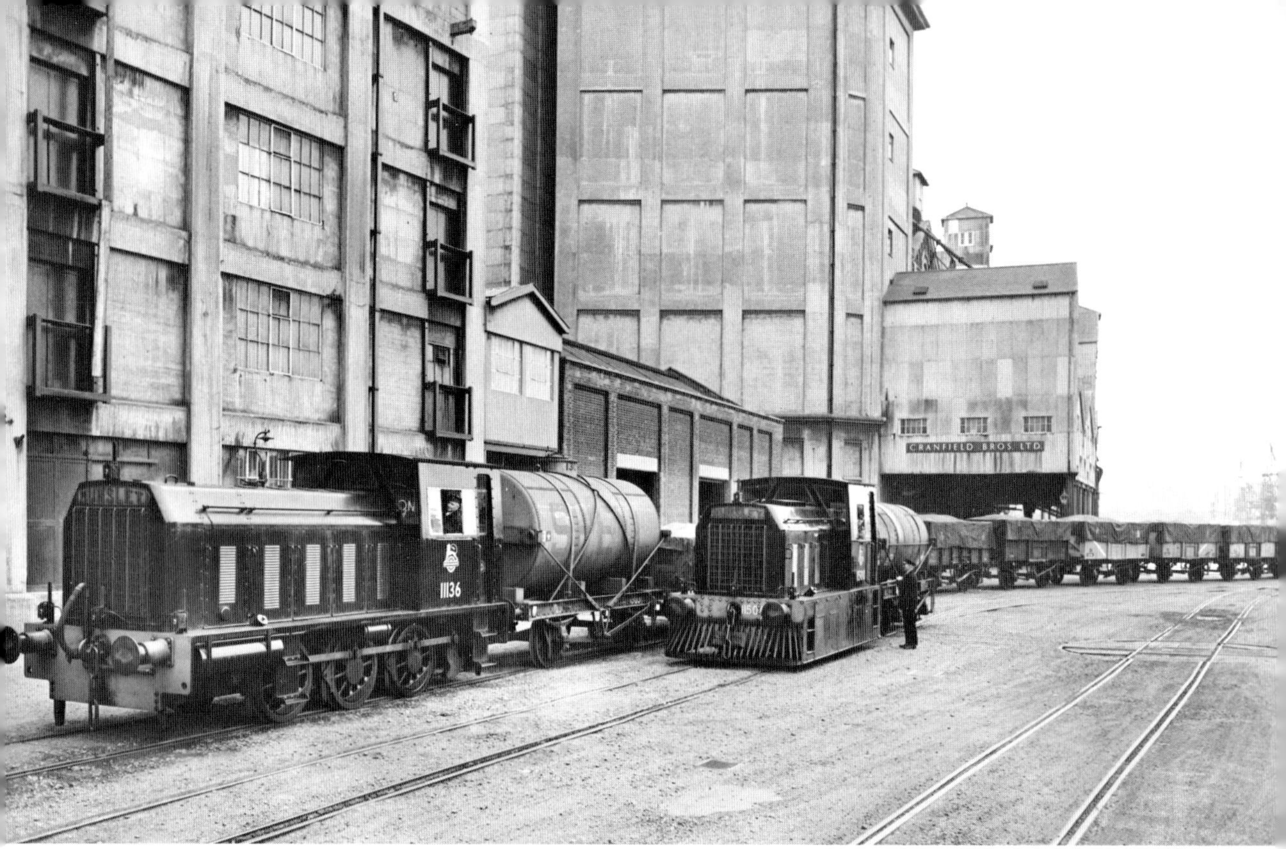
CRANFIELD BROS LTD
11136

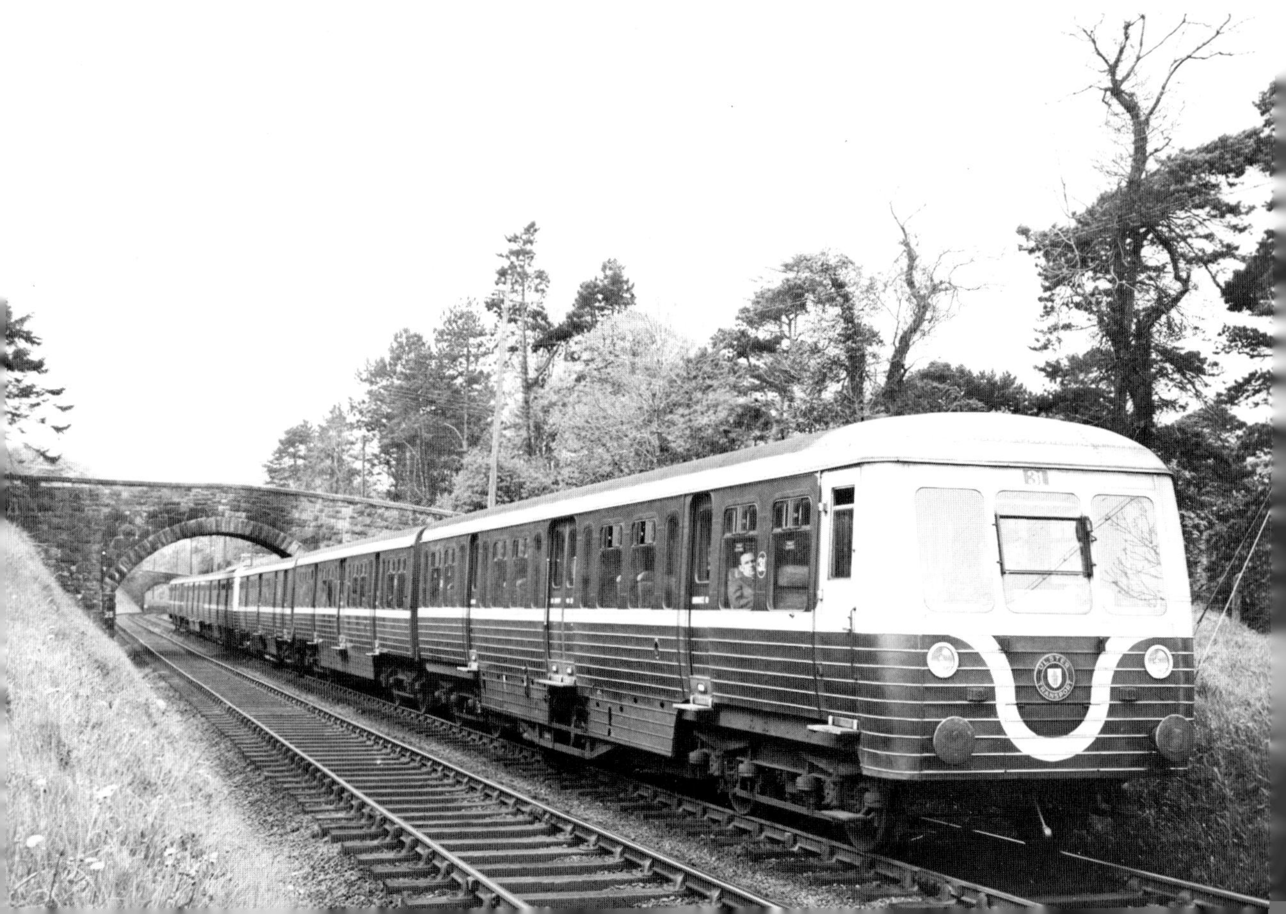
31

Above left: Products of the pre-Modernisation Plan diesel shunter
building programme. Two Hunslet-built examples, a 204hp 0-6-0 (left)
and a 153hp 0-4-0 (right), in Ipswich Docks in the early 1950s.

Left: Much experience had been gained across in Ireland with
underfloor-engined diesel railcars, such as these Ulster Transport
Authority multi-engined 3-coach sets, two of which approach Craigavad
on the Belfast-Bangor line./*NIR*

Above: A glance at other people's experience: a Brush Bagnall 0-6-0
diesel-electric shunter built for the Steel Company of Wales — an
indication that industrial users were moving to diesel power./*Brush*

Right: English Electric's Strand Road, Preston Works in 1955 with
assorted diesel and electric motive power under construction.
Foreground, a main line locomotive for New Zealand, a South African
electric locomotive behind, Bo-Bo units for Nigeria, diesel shunters for
overseas and, of course, *Deltic*./*GEC*

3
The Modernisation Plan

In October 1953 the Railway Executive was abolished, by the Transport Act of 1952, and Area Boards were set up which were directly responsible to the British Transport Commission. Riddles retired on the same date. He had been closely involved in organisation and reorganisation since 1939, and felt he could not face it all over again, particularly under a Transport Commission headed by non-railwaymen who could know little of the job and would have to be taught.[1]

Under the Railway Executive all the officers in charge of the mechanical and electrical engineering establishments in the Regions owed direct allegiance to Riddles; but under the new organisation the Regional departmental officers who had been responsible to a member of the Executive now came under their Regional Manager. However, the major technical and professional matters of their departments were reserved by the Commission, and controlled by the officer concerned on the British Railways Central Staff. With the disappearance of the Member for Mechanical and Electrical Engineering, these two responsibilities were divided at BTC headquarters, though they remained exercised by one man in each Region. Bond was designated Chief Officer (Mechanical Engineering), a title which was later changed to Chief Mechanical Engineer. In each Region there was a Mechanical & Electrical Engineer (later changed to Chief Mechanical & Electrical Engineer) who was responsible technically for these two activities to Bond and Warder (who had been appointed Chief Electrical Engineer) respectively. This worked satisfactorily because Bond and Warder were friends with a common outlook on these matters, but the organisation was faulty because it depended on personalities.[2]

In 1953 Bond and Warder reported directly to the Commission; but in 1955 the Chairman, General Sir Brian Robertson, interposed between the Commission and its Divisions a body of senior officers at headquarters known as the General Staff. The chief officers of the British Railways Central Staff, who, with the six Regions, constituted the Railway Division, were now to be responsible to the Commission through the General Staff, dropping thereby from the second to the third level of management. Bond, for instance, reported to the one Engineer on the General Staff, who was designated Technical Adviser.[3]

Early in 1954 the British Transport Commission appointed a committee of chief officers, of whom Bond was one, to submit proposals for the modernisation and re-equipment of the railways, on the assumption that it would be possible to start implementing their proposals within five years and complete them in fifteen. After six months of intensive work they produced the Modernisation Plan. This was accepted by the Commission and published in December 1954 as a booklet entitled *Modernisation and Re-equipment of British Railways.*[4]

The future motive power of the railways formed a considerable part of the Plan, and under 'Methods of Traction' the booklet said: 'The Commission have decided that major changes in the forms of motive power on British Railways must be effected, involving a widespread changeover from steam to electricity and diesel power.' They considered that these changes would lead to major economies in operation, and they proposed 'to build no new express passenger or suburban steam locomotives after the 1956 programme, and to terminate the building of all new steam locomotives within a few years.' The Commission cited the advantages of the steam locomotive, which had served the railways so well, with its low first cost, simplicity, robustness, and long life, but added that many factors indicated that the end of the steam era was at hand. These included the growing shortage of large coal suitable for locomotives, demands for reduction in air pollution and greater cleanliness in trains and railway stations, and the need for better acceleration. Attention was drawn also to the difficulties of attracting labour to the hard tasks of firing, cleaning, and servicing locomotives, and the wastefulness of such labour. The validity of some of these arguments is open to doubt. Those who remember the cleanliness of trains and stations in the golden years of the steam railway might well maintain that standards have deteriorated rather than the reverse. And it is difficult to believe that having a second man in a diesel locomotive doing nothing is less wasteful than the labour of the fireman in a steam locomotive – the latter at least gets some exercise!

Electrification was considered the ideal solution, because of its reliability, good acceleration, cleanliness, and (given sufficient traffic) economy in operation. Diesel traction, however, offered many of the advantages of electricity in cleanliness, acceleration, and uniform standard of performance. It had the further advantage in that the change from steam did not entail important civil engineering or signal works. On the lines of heaviest traffic, on the other hand, the potential economies were less with diesel traction than with electric.

The cost of a diesel locomotive, at the time of the report, was about two-and-a-half to three times that of a steam locomotive of equivalent power, and therefore, to yield economic results, diesel locomotives would have to be available for nearly as much of their time in service as was theoretically possible.

It was agreed that there was no question of choosing between electrical and diesel traction, but rather of combining the two to the best advantage. There was a wide and accepted field for electrification in surburban services; there was also a wide range of main line services with a density of traffic which might justify electric traction, but the volume of civil and signal engineering works involved limited the mileage that could be completed within the period covered by the Plan. That mileage had been provided for, but on the rest of the principal main line services it was intended to introduce diesel traction as quickly as possible. The main lines which it was intended should be electrified were those from King's Cross to Doncaster and Leeds and, possibly, York; and from Euston to Birmingham and through Crewe to Liverpool and Manchester. A subsidiary project linked Liverpool to Ipswich, and included the Clacton, Harwich, and Felixstowe branches.

As regards diesel traction, a start had already been made in replacing steam services by diesel-powered trains, ranging from single units to six-coach formations, in various parts of the country. A much wider extension of diesel mutliple-unit working was planned which would include three principal types of services: city-to-city express, secondary and cross-country routes, and branch lines. Diesel traction was regarded as a half-way house to electrification; providing many of the advantages of the latter, but without the engineering works that it entailed.

It was proposed to invest substantially in main line diesel locomotives, starting immediately, with the object of changing over as soon as possible from steam to diesel in certain specified areas. It should thus be possible to get the maximum economy through the closing of steam motive power depots and to find out the costs of operating diesel units by themselves without the complication of two forms of traction. It was intended to standardise design as much as possible.

By the end of the period covered by the plan, that is 1970, about 2,500 main line locomotives should be in use. It was intended that on the Western Region, for example, all steam working should be eliminated west of Newton Abbot and that diesel units based in that area should haul a large proportion of passenger and freight trains from the West to London and Bristol and back. On the Southern Region diesel locomotives would replace steam between Waterloo and Exeter, and between Waterloo and Southampton, and on to Bournemouth and Weymouth. For these two schemes some 200 main line diesel locomotives would be required, replacing over 300 steam locomotives. Changes to diesel traction in other areas would be carried out progressively.

There were some 19,000 steam locomotives, of which a substantial number were of modern design. A steam locomotive had a useful life of some 40 years, and careful planning would be needed to ensure that, as the existing stock was replaced gradually by diesel or electric power, it was still used to the best advantage. Types for condemnation would therefore be selected carefully so as to eliminate the less efficient as quickly as possible, as well as those small classes for which it would not be economical to maintain spares.

Bond, of course, had been a party to this plan, but he rightly resented that the Transport Commission, in the way they presented the Plan with a great deal of publicity, implied that the Railway Executive had done nothing during the previous six years towards restoring railway services to their traditionally high standards. As he points out, modernisation is, or should be, a continuing process, and the Railway Executive had gone a long way towards renewing locomotives, rolling stock, and other equipments, and had their own plan for the many things that needed to be done but which had to wait until Government funds were available.[5]

In the change of motive power Bond was faced with a more formidable problem than any previous Chief Mechanical Engineer; for this was not a matter of just improving existing motive power but of introducing an entirely new kind together with all the arrangements for maintenance and training. Furthermore, for Bond, a lover of the steam locomotive, there was added the sadness that it should be he who was to preside over its disappearance. He had had, however, a great interest in diesel locomotives ever since he had been personally involved in the building of LMS No 10000.[6]

Valuable experience had been gained from the performance in traffic of the seven existing diesel locomotives, and this was of considerable assistance when it came to writing specifications for the trial locomotives that would have to be ordered. These would obviously have to cover the whole range of the traffic worked by the various classes of steam locomotives. It was decided that there should be three power groups (later increased to five) with engines ranging from 800hp to 2,000hp. This latter figure was not chosen as the maximum desirable but because at that time there was no locomotive engine of higher power available in a fully developed form. Axle loads were restricted by the Chief Civil Engineer to a maximum of 20 tons, because although 22.5 tons had been allowed on each coupled axle of a steam locomotive, experience from the United States suggested that the heavily loaded small diameter bogie wheels of a diesel locomotive imposed much higher stresses on the track. A range of between 16 and 20 tons was therefore specified, together with wheel spacing, overall dimensions, and total weight which would allow the diesels as wide a route availability as the steam locomotives they would replace. The large locomotives were to have a maximum speed of 90 mile/h and the smaller ones 75 mile/h.

Except for the unconventional Fell locomotive, all the existing main line diesel locomotives on British Railways had electric transmission and Bond was disposed to favour this type as the standard. However, the West German Railways had adopted hydraulic and hydromechanical transmission and claimed that this resulted in locomotives that were cheaper in first cost, lighter for a given power, and cheaper to maintain. Furthermore, at the end of 1953 there had been conversations with the North British Locomotive Company, who had taken out licences for the manufacture of MAN high speed engines and Voith hydraulic transmissions. On their own initiative the firm produced designs for 1,000hp and 2,000hp diesel-hydraulic locomotives which would meet British Railways' general requirements.[7]

At the end of 1954, following the acceptance by the British Transport Commission of the report by the Chief Officers, an initial programme for 174 main line diesel locomotives, submitted by Bond, was approved. These were to undergo trials for the period of three years which Bond had said was essential. At the end of that time he considered that sufficient knowledge should have been acquired to decide on standard makes and types.

Invitations to tender in accordance with Bond's and Warder's specification, were sent out to all British locomotive firms, as well as to three in the United States, one in Canada, and one in Australia. The response to this was overwhelming, with over 200 separate proposals to be studied. Deciding on what should be tried and who should build the locomotives was no easy task, particularly because so few British firms had experience in this field; English Electric being a notable exception. One obvious solution would have been to order a number of locomotives from the experienced General Motors of the United States, as was done later by CIE, the Irish Transport Company, but there were two objections to this. British firms would have been deprived of a 'shop window' to show overseas buyers what their products could do, and, in any case, General Motors never allowed their locomotives or engines to be built under licence in a foreign country.

At the beginning of 1955 Bond took Smeddle, CM&EE of the Western Region, and a party to Germany to assess the merits of diesel-hydraulic traction. He came to the conclusion that some high powered diesel-hydraulic locomotives should be ordered, but that electric transmission, with which both British Railways and British manufacturers had most experience, should predominate in initial orders.[8] The North British Locomotive Company were given a contract for six 1,000hp and five 2,000hp diesel-hydraulic locomotives and Swindon were given authority to build three German-type chassis under licence, each with two 1,000hp Maybach-Mekydro power equipments.[9]

In order to get breadth of experience, the orders for the 174 locomotives included seven makes of engines, eight variants of transmission, and mechanical parts from seven locomotive builders. English Electric having by far

the greatest experience, as much as possible was ordered from them; but to get the numbers needed it was necessary to place larger orders than wished with less experienced manufacturers. The quoted delivery periods for these locomotives varied between 15 months and two years. In fact, this was barely long enough to arrange fuelling and maintenance at motive power depots, equipment at main works for heavy repairs, and the training of footplate and maintenance staff.[10]

Of the 174 locomotives, 160 were to have electric transmission, and 14 hydraulic or mechanical hydraulic. The former were to comprise 40 of 600-1,000hp, 100 of 1,000-1,250hp, and 20 of 2,000hp or over. Of these, 20 in the medium power range and 10 in the high power were to be designed and built by British Railways. All the 14 diesel-hydraulics were allotted to the Western Region, who had pressed for them because they did not want to face the problems of setting up an electric organisation which they had never had. The Region did not apparently realise that diesel-hydraulic locomotives have a mass of electrics in their control systems.[11]

Before any of these locomotives were delivered, however, a very remarkable diesel-electric locomotive was submitted by English Electric for test on British Railways. In 1955 English Electric built a Co-Co type locomotive powered by two Napier-Deltic opposed piston engines each of 1,650hp, making it the most powerful single unit diesel-electric locomotive. There were three banks of cylinders, each bank of six cylinders forming one side of an inverted equilateral triangle with a crankshaft at each apex. There were opposed pistons in each cylinder, and the engine, unusually in a diesel-electric locomotive, ran at the high speed of 1,500rev/min. Since this engine form was described as 'deltic', the locomotive was named *Deltic*. It was accepted for trials by British Railways in October 1955, and was tested initially on fast freight trains on the London Midland Region. Two months later it was working express passenger trains between Euston and Liverpool, and from October 1956 it was running very successfully on regular express passenger workings over the West Coast main line. The results of these trials led to smaller locomotives with the Deltic engine being included amongst the first 174 ordered. In January 1959 the *Deltic* was transferred to the Eastern Region.

The 174 diesel locomotives ordered were as follows:

Mechanical parts	Engine	Transmission	Wheel arrangement	No Ordered
English Electric	EE 1,000hp	EE electric	Bo-Bo	20
English Electric	EE 1,100hp (Deltic)	EE electric	Bo-Bo	10
English Electric	EE 2,000hp	EE electric	1Co-Co1	10
Clayton	Paxman 800hp	BTH electric	Bo-Bo	10
British Railways	Sulzer 1,160hp	ETH electric	Bo-Bo	20
British Railways	Sulzer 2,300hp	CP electric	1Co-Co1	10
British Railways	Maybach 2,200hp	Mekydro hydro-mechanical	B-B	3
North British	Paxman 800hp	BTH electric	B-Bo	10
North British	MAN 1,000hp	GEC electric	Bo-Bo	10
North British	MAN 1,000hp	Voith hydraulic	Bo-Bo	6

Mechanical parts	Engine	Transmission	Wheel arrangement	No Ordered
North British	MAN 2,000hp	Voith hydraulic	A1A-A1A	5
Birmingham RC&W	Sulzer 1,160hp	CP electric	Bo-Bo	20
Brush	Mirlees 1,250hp	Brush electric	A1A-A1A	20
MV	Crossley 1,200hp	MV electric	Co-Bo	20

Note: BTH, British Thomson-Houston; CP, Crompton Parkinson; GEC, General Electric Company; MV, Metropolitan-Vickers.

The diesel engines ordered presented an interesting variety. English Electric's medium-speed engines were well tried and reliable. This could claim to be the oldest firm in the locomotive business because Robert Stephenson & Company was one of the constituents, and that establishment was founded in 1823. The high speed Deltic engine was manufactured by D. Napier & Son, another constituent, and was something of an innovation because it had been developed as a marine engine. Sulzer is one of the oldest names in diesel traction and the firm had a high reputation for reliability. The first main line diesel locomotive of all, built for the Prussian State Railways in 1912, had an engine constructed by Gebr Sulzer AG of Winterthur, Switzerland. The British firm of Paxman introduced its first diesel engines into railway traction in 1930, and since 1951 they had been operating very successfully in Ceylon. The Crossley engine was a two-stroke engine, and Bond was interested to see how it compared with the four-stroke engines. MAN is the abbreviation for the German firm of Maschinenfabrik Augsburg-Nurnberg AG. The world's first diesel engine was built by Maschinenfabrik Augsburg AG between 1893 and 1897. Shortly after this the firm amalgamated with Maschinenbau AG Nurnberg, and the present title was adopted. The North British Locomotive Company had made arrangements to manufacture MAN engines under licence.

English Electric was the only firm building the mechanical parts and electrical transmissions as well as the engines. The North British Locomotive Company was one of the greatest names in steam locomotive building, but the main line diesel was a new venture. In 1889 Brush Electrical Machines Limited had been formed with the acquisition of the Falcon Works in Loughborough, builders of railway and tram locomotives and rolling stock. Brush continued building on similar lines till 1914, but concentrated on electric traction after World War I. The firm began building diesel locomotives in 1948, when H. G. Ivatt joined Brush as a consultant after retiring from the railway.

Metropolitan-Vickers had been long established in the building of electric locomotives and British Thomson-Houston and the General Electric Company were both well-known suppliers of motors and other equipment for electric railways. BTH and Metrovick had in fact merged some years previously as Associated Electrical Industries (AEI), but they still functioned as separate entitites. (GEC eventually took over AEI; it later acquired English Electric and ultimately Paxman.)

The Clayton Equipment Company, recipient of an order for a solitary type of locomotive, had been incorporated in 1931 to manufacture locomotives, railcars and other engineering products; though its antecedents went back to 1842, to Nathaniel Clayton and his partner Joseph Shuttleworth. In 1957 Claytons were acquired by International Combustion (Holdings) Ltd, but continued to operate as a semi-autonomous establishment until 1969. Crompton Parkinson were fiercely independent manufacturers of electric motors and generators, standing out against the great combines. In due course, however, they were taken over by Hawker-Siddeley, as also was Brush. The Birmingham Railway Carriage & Wagon Company had been building railway rolling stock since the 19th century.

It will be noted that Bond had sound reasons for his choice of manufacturers and components for his trial locomotives, and it would be difficult to suggest ways in which they could have been bettered.

Notes
1 Riddles, R. A.; Information to the Author
2 Bond, R. C.; Information to the Author
3 Bond Roland C.; *A Lifetime with Locomotives;* Cambridge, Goose & Son, 1975, pp285-231
4 ibid, p233
5 ibid, pp234-5
6 ibid, pp238-9, and information to the Author
7 Cox, E. S.; *Locomotive Panorama vol.2;* Ian Allan Ltd, 1966, p122, Bond, op cit, p240
8 ibid, p240, and information to Author
9 Cox, op cit, p122 Bond, information to the Author
10 Bond, op cit, pp240-1 and information to the Author
11 Bond, information to the Author

Top: Public opinion had turned against steam in ths early 1950s, encouraged by the pollution emanating from sheds such as Camden, seen here in September 1950./*BR*

Above: An early example of BR's diesel multiple-unit fleet, a 2-car Derby 'lightweight' unit, leaving Leeds Central for Harrogate. /*Kenneth Field*

Left: It was intended that the Modernisation Plan diesels would banish steam from particular areas. High on the list was the WR main line west of Newton Abbot. Here 'Manor' 4-6-0 No 7814 *Fringford Manor* and 'Castle' 4-6-0 No 4075 *Cardiff Castle* do battle past Tigley box in September 1957, on the eve of dieselisation. /*A.R. Butcher*

Above: The changeover from steam to diesel affected workshops as well as sheds. Stratford Works' repair shop is altered to handle the new form of traction.

Left: Diesel-hydraulic main line locomotives were to feature as part of the Modernisation Plan. Brand-new North British 2,000hp AIA-AIA No D600 begins trials on the Scottish Region./*North British/Mitchell Library*

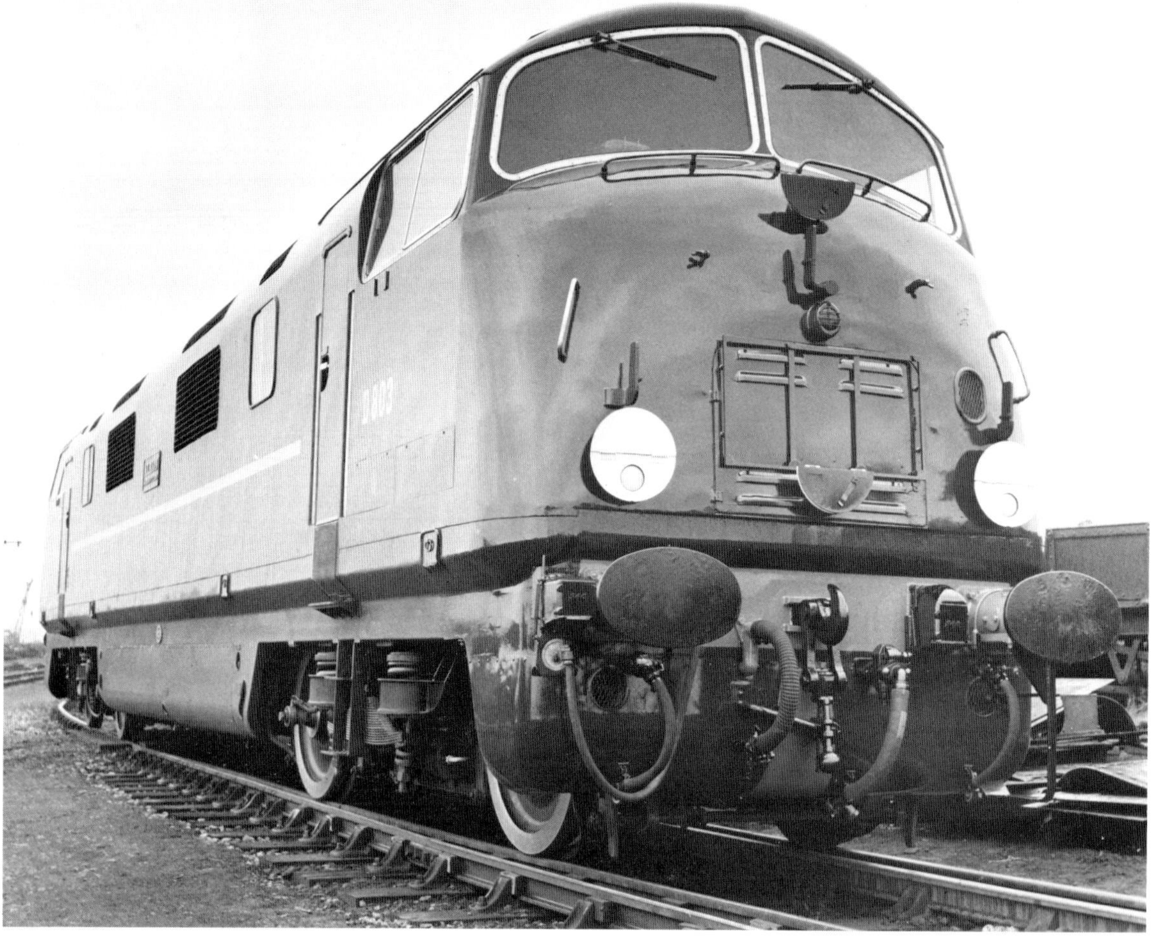
D803

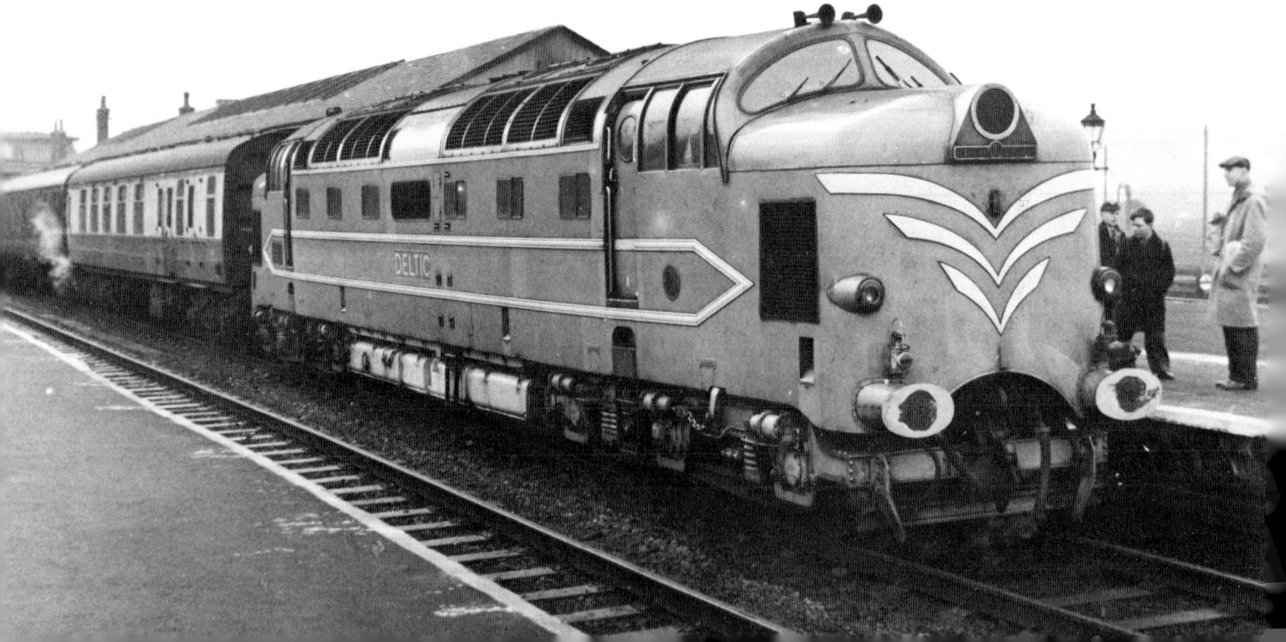
DELTIC

Left: The first of the main series of Swindon-built 2,000hp twin-engined Bo-Bo diesel-hydraulics, No D803 *Albion,* at Swindon in March 1959./*Sam Lambert*

Below left: At a later stage of its trials on BR, the prototype *Deltic* waits at Grantham on a down East Coast express on 21 February 1959.

Above right: English Electric's Type 1 800hp design, built totally by the company – diesel engine, electrical equipment and all mechanical parts./*Sam Lambert*

Centre right: Brush entered the picture as Brush Bagnall, so far as the Modernisation Plan diesels were concerned. One of the 1,250hp Type 2s takes shape at Loughborough with the Mirlees JVS12T engine in place and coupled to a Brush generator./*Brush*

Below: The finished result. D5500, the pioneer Brush Type 2, does its best to brighten up Liverpool Street station on 13 November 1957, when working its first booked train, the 10.36 to Clacton./*BR*

Above: A pair of the AEI/Clayton/Paxman Type 1 800hp Bo-Bos in service on the ER. */GEC*

Left: Crewe Works was adapted to production of the Type 2 Bo-Bo diesel-electrics in the late 1950s, a type latterly known as Class 24. During 1958 one of these is in an advanced stage of construction./*BR*

Above: A typical small diesel shunter, a 204hp 0-4-0 diesel mechanical of 1958, built by Andrew Barclay of Kilmarnock./*Hunslet*

Centre left: A major part of the Modernisation Plan was devoted to diesel railcars. One of the ubiquitous Metro-Cammell design of cars, in this case a 3-car unit for the North Eastern Region, delivered in 1960./*Metro-Cammell*

Below left: A Rolls-Royce engined Derby-built 3-car dmu for the Eastern Region./*Rolls-Royce*

Top: D. Wickham's diesel railbus No SC79969 for the Scottish Region, powered by a Meadows 6-cylinder diesel engine./*D. Wickham & Co*

Above: The Modernisation Plan had envisaged 1,500V dc electrification such as on the Manchester-Sheffield-Wath lines. No 26020, one of the system's Bo-Bos, at Penistone West on an up freight in February 1955. /*K. Field*

4
The Road Ahead

It was not till May 1957 that the first of the 174 diesel locomotives was delivered to British Railways. In the meantime it was necessary to consider the factors which should govern selection of the types to be standardised and the matters that would have to be taken into account in deciding future policy. Bond accordingly instructed his staff to prepare a paper on these lines. This was issued by the Chief Mechanical Engineer's Office, British Railways Central Staff, in July 1956 and sent to all Regional General Managers.

The 'Preliminary Comments' included the following points:

'Apart from shunting, where two types of locomotive have already become firmly established, namely 200hp and 350hp on six coupled wheels, the number of types which will be required to operate British Railways, their power range and their leading features have yet to be established as a result of practical experience.

'However strong the trend towards multiple-unit train sets, the separate locomotive must remain an important element in our motive power, firstly for the obvious reason that freight forms the greater part of the traffic pattern on all Regions except the Southern, and secondly because the need to ensure high locomotive utilisation will demand mixed traffic working, part passenger, part freight, by a considerable proportion of the stock.

'As with other forms of motive power, technical and operating requirements, ideal from one point of view, will be found to conflict with others, equally desirable from a different point of view. These conflicts will have to be resolved. For example, on the one hand is the desire to use the changeover to a new form of power to rationalise provision of locomotives down to a single standard unit, of such power and dimensions that it will meet all traffic needs by multiplication or division under multiple-unit working. On the other, the high cost of diesel units and especially the higher cost of several smaller units as against that of one larger one, indicates a need to relate size of locomotive closely to the various operating conditions which have to be met, circumstances leading to selection of a number of locomotive types rather than a single standard.

'As a practical first step, provision for 174 main line diesel locomotives has been authorised, divided into three power groups as under:

Type A – 600-1000hp
Type B – 1000-1250hp
Type C – 2000hp or over . . .

'The makes and types finally selected will enable operating experiments and trials to be carried out over the next three years . . .

'Without waiting that length of time, however, certain basic facts can be established, and world trends in engine and locomotive design can be examined so that a preview of the kind of locomotive pattern likely to emerge can be established.'

The above comments are important because they show the trials of the 174 locomotives were intended to determine not only the most reliable components, but also the sizes of locomotives required to work the various traffics of British Railways and the proportions of each.

The paper pointed out that the bulk of traffic on the main lines at that time was being hauled by nine power groups of steam locomotives, and that three of the reasons that had led to as many as nine power classes would apply also, in some measure, to diesels. These were:

a A number of different axle loads were necessary to exploit the maximum allowed on different routes;
b Specific fuel costs became excessive when too heavy an engine had to operate a light train; and
c The increased capital costs of a large locomotive would weight the operating costs unduly if it were used for duties well within the capacity of a smaller one.

There were, indeed, two conflicting requirements: the biggest engine that the route would allow, and the smallest engine that would work the traffic.

However, there were certain differences in the respective characteristics of the two forms of motive power. In tractive performance a diesel exerted considerably more drawbar pull than a steam locomotive of comparable power at slow speeds and rather less at high speeds; so that diesels could not conform exactly to steam power classifications. For instance: at 10mile/h a 1,500hp diesel locomotive had the same drawbar pull on the level as a Class 8 steam engine; but at 15mile/h it exerted the pull of a Class 7 and at 20mile/h that of a Class 6; then between 30 and 50mile/h it was only equivalent to a Class 5, and above 60mile/h it was only equal to a good Class 4. Thus, on the LMS, No 10000 would have had the drawbar pull of a 'Duchess' Pacific at starting, but only that of a Midland Compound when in full flight. Another important point of difference was that a steam locomotive retained a reservoir capacity in its boiler which permitted exceptional effort for a short period; but it was not advisable to operate a diesel locomotive, under any circumstances, above its rated engine horsepower. Drawbar pull/speed curves showed that a group of diesel locomotives of between 500 and 2,500 engine hp would cover the same kind of performance range (although different in detail) as steam locomotives between Classes 2 and 9, and thus could replace the existing steam traction. But as one of the objectives of the Modernisation Plan was to prepare for higher operating performance in the future, higher powers would eventually be necessary. A diesel locomotive could never attain the specific power output of an electric locomotive of the same weight because it was limited by the capacity of its own prime mover. It could however be designed and used to produce considerably more power than given by any existing steam locomotive. For example: at a constant speed of 75mile/h a Class 8 Pacific would produce on the level a drawbar pull of 6,500lb; two 1,500hp diesel locomotives in multiple could produce 7,500lb; two 2,000hp diesels 10,500lb; and a single 3,400hp 'Deltic' 11,800lb. At lower speeds the diesel superiority was considerably greater. A point which does not of course emerge from these comparisons is that the diesel's much greater acceleration enables it to reach a high speed much more quickly than a steam engine, and the diesel scores again when it comes to hill climbing.

Except for shunting, the modern diesel locomotive is carried on bogies, and a number of weight considerations affected their design. Route availability depended on axle weight, total weight, and axle spacing on both individual locomotives and the adjacent end axles of locomotives coupled together. In addition, American diesel experience, as well as theoretical investigation, indicated that if bogie wheels were smaller than a certain ratio of diameter to weight carried, high rail stresses would result which could lead in time to rail fracture. Since there is a limit to the size of a bogie wheel, this would limit in turn the maximum axle weight. The necessary power could of course be obtained with light axle loads by either increasing the number of axles on a locomotive or by working two or more locomotives in multiple units. However, every additional pair of axles increases locomotive weight, capital cost, and the annual charges for a given horsepower; factors which favour a single locomotive with the fewest axles that will do the job, ie two four-wheeled bogies.

A formula proposed by the Civil Engineers was that the axle weight in tons divided by the wheel diameter in feet should not exceed 4.5. This would be a very difficult figure to meet, and the CME's Office paper insisted that some tolerance would be necessary, as the following table shows:

Max axle load	Route mileage available	Civil Engineers' minimum diameter
13	Nearly all	2ft 5in
16	All, except small branches	3ft 7in
18	90% passenger or freight	4ft 0in
20	83% passenger, 48% freight	4ft 7in
22½	Certain main trunk routes only	5ft 1in

The largest bogie wheel that would clear satisfactorily an underframe carrying a large diesel engine was about 4ft 0in, so that considerable tolerance on the above figures

would be needed for an axle load of 20 tons. (In fact the Chief Civil Engineer seems to have been very tolerant indeed, for the axle loads and bogie wheel diameters of the large locomotives ordered were: BR/Sulzer 1Co-Co1, axle load 18 tons 16cwt, wheel diameter 3ft 9in; English Electric 1Co-Co1, axle load 18 tons, wheel diameter 3ft 9in; NBL/MAN A1A-A1A, axle load 20 tons, wheel diameter 3ft 7in; BR/Maybach Bo-Bo, axle load 19 tons 15cwt, wheel diameter 3ft 3½in.)

As regards riding qualities, the maximum speeds of the time were in the region of 90 mile/h, but consideration had to be given to the higher speeds of the future. Plenty of six-wheeled bogies already existed that would give good riding at 90 mile/h, but no British four-wheeled bogie had so far proved its good riding at this speed. For speeds above 90 mile/h experiment and development would be necessary for both four- and six-wheeled bogies, and it was proposed that soon after delivery of the 174 main line diesel locomotives, alternative high-speed bogies would be fitted to a few of them for trial.

In the range of 1,000 − 3,600hp, which covered all main line requirements that could be readily foreseen, any power needed could be met either by a single locomotive or by locomotives in multiple. The latter practice had been widely favoured in the United States; firstly because it provided power suitable for use over almost any routes; secondly because the locomotives could be split into their components for flexible operating; and thirdly quantity production of a single type allowed price reduction and a limited number of standardised spares. On the other hand, two or more small locomotives cost more than one large one, and the increased locomotive length could cause difficulties at short platforms and sidings. However, where a variety of duties having different power needs could be grouped to provide high utilisation, the resulting savings might outweigh the increased capital and running costs of two or more locomotives. As there seemed no way of assessing in advance the merits of these two locomotive conceptions, any outline plan for future standard types should be so phrased as to allow either or both to be employed. The trial period with the 174 locomotives on order and completion of traffic surveys would eventually make it possible to state Region by Region the most favourable combination of units. (This was, of course, yet another important reason for the extended trial of the 174 locomotives).

The development of diesel engines was still fluid, and there was a visible trend away from the well-established low speed and relatively heavy engines of proved reliability towards the lighter engines of high speed, which still had to prove themselves reliable. Electric transmissions might be made lighter, and hydraulic and hydro-mechanical transmissions offered a substantial reduction in weight. It was necessary to distinguish, therefore, between the locomotives to be designed in the immediate future, which, because of the demands for proved reliability, would probably have the heavier engines, and the probable designs of five years hence when lighter engines and transmissions might have proved their worth.

While it was recognised that reliability was the first and

essential requirement, the need for weight reduction came a close second in implementing the Modernisation Plan, and while maintaining for the time being a 'bread and butter' series of locomotives, bold development was desirable towards the second stage.

The above were the highlights of a paper that included a great deal more of detail; but they show the difficulties in planning a complete change in motive power when there was little past experience to provide a guide. Furthermore, owing to the rapid development of diesel practice and design, there was as yet no firm planning ground – Bond and his team were standing metaphorically on shifting sands. Amongst the things that had to be decided were:

a The best types of locomotives for immediate use;

b Whether working in multiple with small locomotives was or was not preferable to using single-unit locomotives of greater power;

c Arising from b, the number of locomotives of different power needed;

d The direction of forward planning for the next generation of diesel locomotives.

Apart from the locos themselves, however, there was the major problem of training staff to operate them and maintain them, as well as the accommodation, equipment, and facilities for that maintenance. How formidable a problem this is can be assessed by the number of countries which have rushed to replace their steam engines by diesels – which now stand idle and broken through lack of the knowledge to drive and maintain them. Three years was none too long a period for both men and machines. It was not to be realised.

In the latter part of 1956, Bond was informed to his horror and dismay that the Transport Commission were abandoning the three year trial period, and were prepared to extend and accelerate the introduction of diesel locomotives as rapidly as production capacity would allow.

The reason for this sudden change of policy was that the railway was in a bad way financially, and the Commission believed that the situation could only be restored by getting rid of steam as quickly as possible.[1] Bond went to see Sir Brian Robertson and pointed out the dangers of giving up the trial period; for it would entail ordering a large number of diesel locomotives before any of them had been tried out. Robertson overruled his protests and told him to go ahead and order the locomotives, adding that all Bond had to do was to ensure that good and reliable locomotives were produced. To this Bond replied that this was the main reason for having the trial period, and that he could not guarantee that locomotives which had never been tested on British Railways were reliable.[2]

Thus before any of the new locomotives had even been delivered, Bond was faced with the task of ordering lots more of them, straight off the drawing board, and before the Regions had made adequate arrangements for main-taining them or for training the staff. The inevitable consequences were unreliable operation and general dissatisfaction.[3]

The Commission had also required that the number of different designs of locomotives should be reduced to a minimum. This, again, was one of the objects of the trial period. However, in order to comply with the Commission's instructions to order locomotives as quickly as possible, Bond and Warder decided to increase the 40 Bo-Bo type diesels being built by British Railways and the Birmingham Carriage & Wagon Company by another 56. These locomotives had the well-tried and reliable Sulzer six-cylinder engine of 1,160hp.

On 30 May 1957 the Secretary-General of the British Transport Commission wrote requesting that the questions involved in limiting the variety of engines, transmissions, control systems and mechanical parts by choice of manufacturer, and in rationalisation of design, should be sent for study and recommendations to the Chief Mechanical & Electrical Engineers of the Regions through the medium of special meetings to be convened by Messrs Bond and Warder. This was a most extraordinary wording, considering that Bond and Warder were the technical superiors of the Regional CM&EEs. As a result of this, however, Bond and Warder held a meeting and the result was embodied in a paper entitled *Main Line Diesel Locomotives: Limitation of Variety*, dated 26 July 1957.

The paper pointed out that the orders so far placed for diesel locomotives had been on the basis of deliberately ordering the widest available variety, with the object of gaining experience. This was in accordance with the recommendations of the Works and Equipment Committee, and it had been the original intention that no further orders should be placed for three years, so that when bulk ordering began a limited selection of types could be selected based upon the results obtained with the locomotives being tested. Without the paper actually saying so, this meant of course that it had always been the intention to limit variety, but under the new policy the problem was what to limit!

The paper continued that within the power ranges envisaged a total of 444 locomotives had been authorised, of which orders had been placed for 230 locomotives or equipment sets. Of these, there were the original 174 authorised in the 1956 and 1957 programmes and the above-mentioned 56 authorised for the 1958 programme. The remainder of the 444 were made up by 116 diesel-hydraulic locomotives authorised in the 1958 Western Region Supplementary Programme and 98 diesel-electric locomotives approved in principle as part of the requirements for the Southern Region Electrification scheme. (These last eventually materialised as the 98 BRCW/Sulzer Type 3 locomotives for the Southern.) More recently, the paper added, enquiries for Type 3 locomotives had been issued and tenders had been received from eight main contractors, with a correspondingly wide range of engines, transmissions, and mechanical parts.

The consideration given by the Commission to the Passenger Traffic Survey had led them to approve the immediate extension and acceleration of the introduction of diesel traction, but with the requirement that there should be the absolute minimum of types and makes.

It had now become necessary, therefore, to recommend the smallest possible range of types, consistent with technical and production considerations, and before any operating experience had been obtained with the locomotives then on order. The only way of doing this was to base recommendations on engineering judgement, knowledge of various firms' products, and the operating experience of other railways. Based on these, the principles governing the recommendations in the paper were as follows:

a The overriding need was for locomotives to be completely reliable.

b Experience in the USA showed that availability and repair were best promoted by as much standardisation as possible.

c But because under British conditions it was impossible to obtain as much as was needed from one firm, it was necessary in the first place to specify more than one power equipment.

d Choice of power equipment would be made in the following order of priority:
   1 Those designed and manufactured in UK
   2 Those of foreign origin but manufactured in UK
   3 Those of foreign design and manufacture already on order for which it might be possible to arrange manufacture in UK.

e The high speed light weight diesel engine of German origin would be confined to the Western Region until experience had been gained with it under BR conditions. For other regions the potentially more reliable medium speed heavier engine would be preferred.

f There would be as much standardisation as possible of renewable parts within the selected locomotive types.

In the light of the above it was recommended that orders placed in the 1959 programme should be as follows, subject to the relation between the Regions' requirements and the production capacity of the firms:

The Transport Commission had mentioned a total of about 500 as desirable for the 1959 programme, and the paper went on to show the extent to which this might be realised within the above table.

The Western Region had proposed for the 1959 programme, 110 locomotives of Types 1 and 2 and 90 of Type 4. They wanted them to have hydraulic transmission, but no decision on this had yet been taken. If the remaining 300 locomotives were distributed amongst the other Regions in proportion to the numbers of each type postulated in the Passenger Traffic Survey, they would amount to 30 Type 1, 90 Type 2, 90 Type 3 and 90 Type 4. These figures, if related to the classes listed in the above table, would call for the following production of power equipments: English Electric, 30 Type 1 and 90 Type 3; Sulzer, 90 Type 2 and 90 Type 4. However, it was known that English Electric had a far greater production capacity than Sulzer (probably more than 150 main line equipments a year), whilst it was unlikely that Sulzer could produce 90 2,200hp engines in a year. It followed that BR would have to design the Type 4 locomotives to take either Sulzer or English Electric engines. English Electric might therefore be asked to build 60 Type 4 engines, leaving Sulzer with 30.

The capacity of English Electric to build complete Type 4 locomotives would depend on whether they were also required to produce 'Deltic' locomotives within the same period. If they were, then it might be desirable to increase the number of Type 4 locomotives built in BR shops, with a corresponding reduction in the number of Type 2s, which could be ordered from a contractor.

As regards the reasons for selecting English Electric and Sulzer engines, it was pointed out that English Electric had the largest experience and productive capacity of any British manufacturer and had the resources to ensure an ultimately reliable job, whilst the Sulzer engine was the best known and most widely used outside the USA, and was of excellent design and workmanship. Paxman engines were proposed as a reserve type and were made by a firm with an excellent factory and good production facilities; but limited experience with their product in the 800-1,000 hp power

All Regions except WR	Engine	Transmission	Mechanical parts
Type 1 1,000hp (BB)	English Electric	English Electric	English Electric
Type 2 1,160hp (BB)	Sulzer	BTH	BR
Type 3 1,700hp (A1A,A1A)	English Electric	English Electric	English Electric
Type 4 2,200hp (1CC1)	Sulzer	Crompton	BR
For WR			
Type 2 1,000hp	NB/MAN	Hydraulic or	NB
Type 4 2,000hp	NB/MAN or Maybach	Electric as may be decided	BR

range had not been entirely satisfactory. Crossley and Mirlees engines were excluded from the recommendations because both engine builders had less experience of traction requirements than the recommended firms. It was a comment to be found well justified.

It was considered that the assessment made in the paper was the best that could be offered until complete information had been received from the Regions as to the number and types of locomotives that they would need. When this information was available, firm figures could be arrived at and discussed with Industry, because the capacity of the different firms would affect not only the division of orders but also the number of firms on whom it would be necessary to call.

In fact discussions with Industry soon showed that it was not possible to adhere as closely as had been hoped to the limitations proposed. There was no difficulty over the English Electric Type 1s, and 128 of these had been built by 1961. Of the Type 2s with Sulzer engines, both British Railways and the Birmingham Railway Carriage & Wagon Company went on building them, but in fewer numbers than needed. As English Electric were not required at the moment to build 'Deltics' they had spare capacity and were asked to build more of their 2,000hp 1Co-Co1 locomotives; whilst BR were to go on building Type 4s with Sulzer engines. An order for Type 3 locomotives of 1,750hp with a Co-Co wheel arrangement was given to English Electric and BRCW were given the order for the 98 Type 3 1,500hp locomotives which, as stated above, had already been approved in principle for the Southern Region. Like BRCW's Type 2s, they were to have Sulzer engines. To meet the demand for Type 2 locomotives, Brush received an order for more of their A1A-A1A locomotives. In spite of the doubts about them, they were to have the Mirlees engines, though uprated from 1,250 to 1,365hp. Presumably there had been second thoughts about Paxman engines as a reserve type.

The Western Region were allowed to have hydraulic and hydro-mechanical transmissions after all. They were embodied in more of the BR type 4s with Maybach engines and the NB Type 2s with MAN engines. But North British also received an order for more of their Type 2 locomotives with MAN engines and electric transmissions.

Towards the end of 1958 Sir Landale Train retired from the British Transport Commission and was succeeded by J. Ratter, the engineer on the General Staff to whom Bond had reported. Bond was promoted to the General Staff in his place and was succeeded by J. F. Harrison as CME in October 1958. Harrison had started his career on the Great Northern Railway and had been a devoted disciple of Sir Nigel Gresley. Nationalisation had probably deprived him of succeeding A. H. Peppercorn as CME of the London & North Eastern Railway. Latterly he had been CM&EE of the London Midland Region.

Shortly before Harrison became CME, Western Region pressure had resulted in the ordering of two new classes of diesel-hydraulic locomotives. These were the Type 4 'Western' class C-C with two 1,350hp Maybach engines, constructed by British Railways, and a Type 3 BB locomotive of 1,700hp with hydro-mechanical transmission, built by Beyer Peacock, and called by them the 'Hymek', in reference to its transmission. Both classes were built, in compliance with the Commission's directive, in quantity without prototypes. However, like the final eight-foot singles of the broad gauge, they were to be the last of a Western deviation from current practice.

Notes

1 Bond Roland C.; *A Lifetime with Locomotives;* Cambridge, Goose & Son, 1975, p244
2 Bond, R. C.; Information to the Author
3 Bond; *A Lifetime with Locomotives*, p245

Below: The diesels take over. One of the Brush Type 2 AIA-AIAs at Stratford, ER./*Sam Lambert*

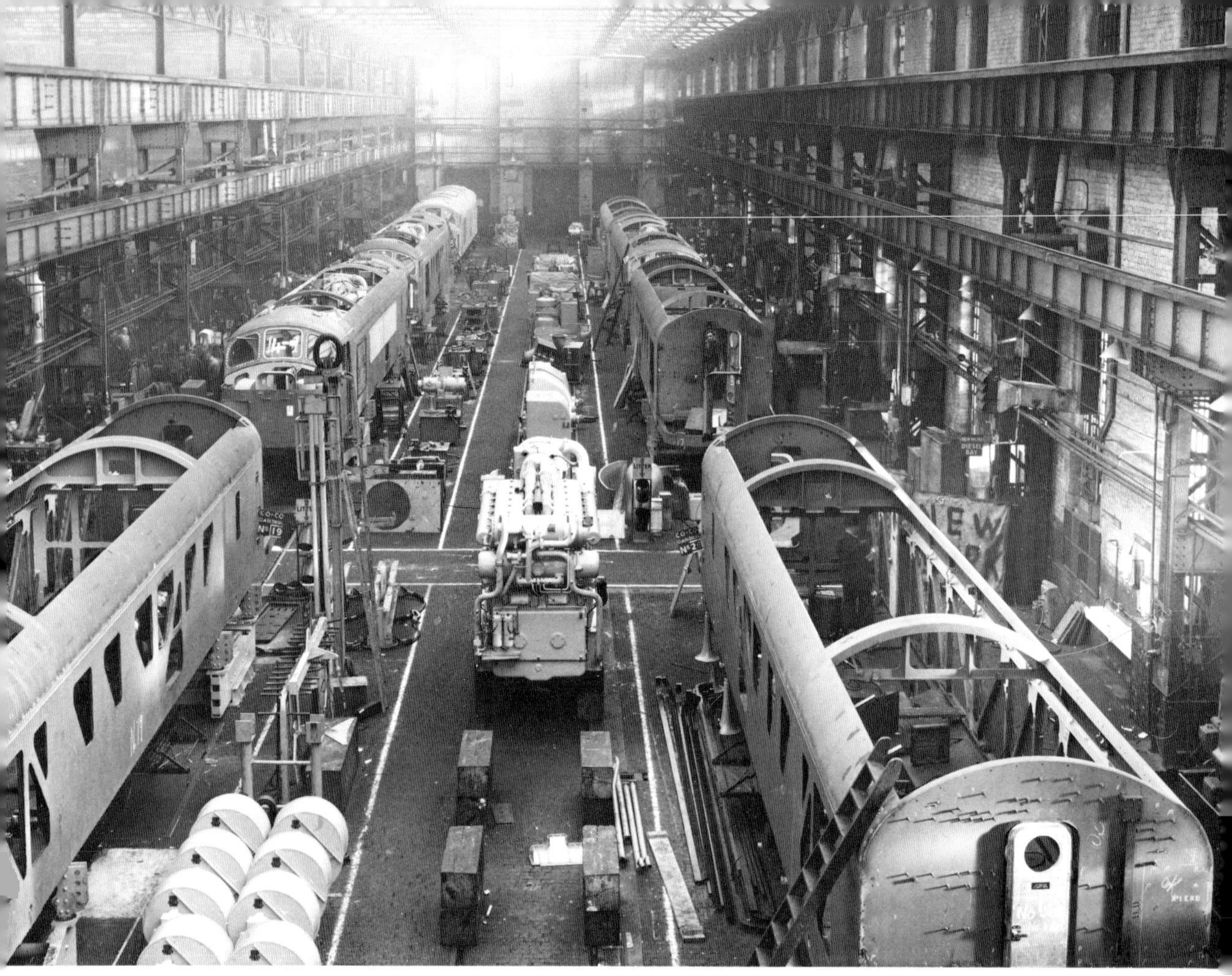

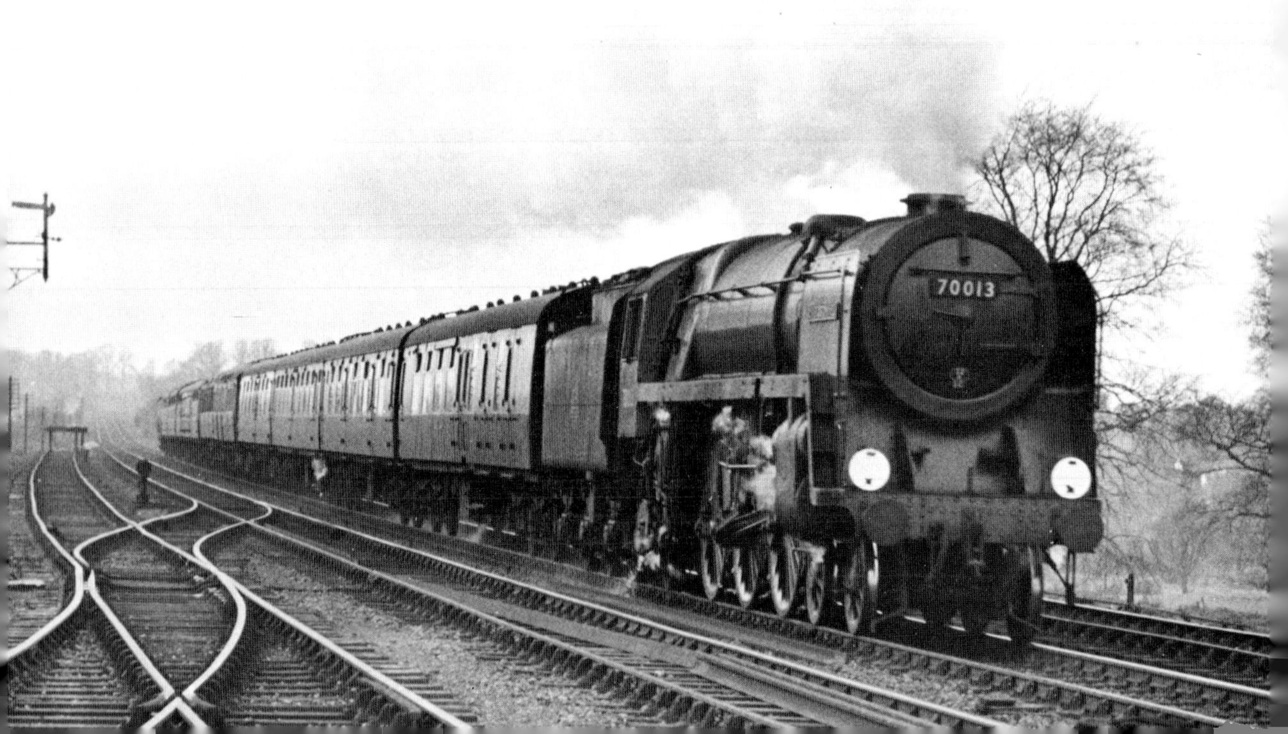
70013

Left: Diesel production in full swing during 1960 at Derby Works; these were to become Class 45s./*BR*

An example of closely matched steam and diesel designs. The 'Britannia' Pacifics could marginally better the English Electric Type 4s on comparable workings with express passenger trains. 'Britannia' No 70013 *Oliver Cromwell (below left)* seems to be making good speed with a Liverpool St-Norwich express near Hatfield Peverel in 1956. An interesting combination of locomotive, train and line – EE Type 4 No D208 *(above)* with the York-Bournemouth train near Bulwell Common, on the GC main line, in October 1958./*D. Swale/J. Head*

Below: The BR/Sulzer Type 4s (Classes 44-46) bear witness to the civil engineers' deliberations of the mid to late 1950s in their wheel arrangement and bogie design./*D.E. Canning*

Above: Many tests were carried out with diesel types well away from their original home territory. Brush Type 2 No D5511 with a train of Minfits on the Edinburgh Suburban line in 1958./*W.S. Sellar*

Below: During the height of diesel locomotive production two BR/Sulzer Type 4 locomotives have their train heating boilers tested outside Crewe Works' paintshop./*J.R. Carter*

Right: Swindon's 2,200hp diesel-hydraulic type with No D827 *Kelly* on a running-in turn from Swindon Works at Badminton on 3 October 1960./*Sam Lambert*

Below right: English Electric's Vulcan Foundry at full stretch in 1960/61 producing 'Deltics' for the East Coast route./*GEC*

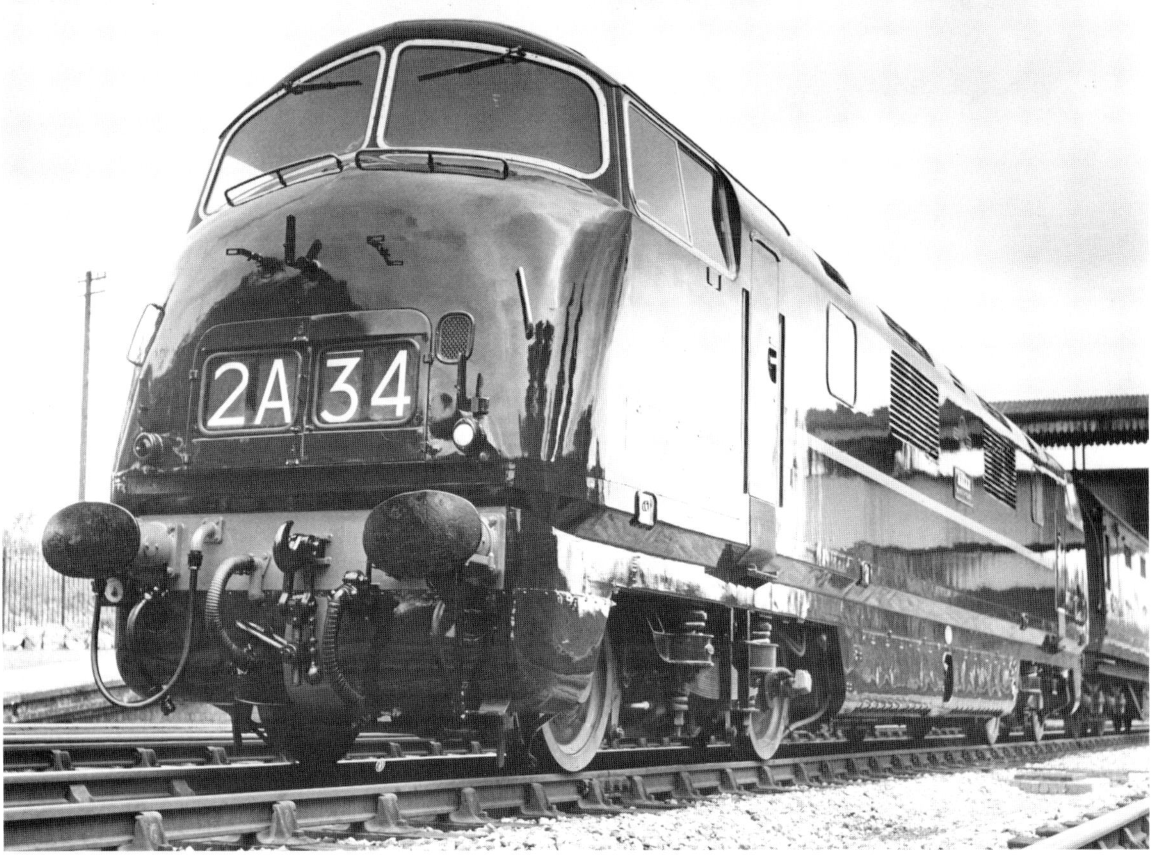
2A34
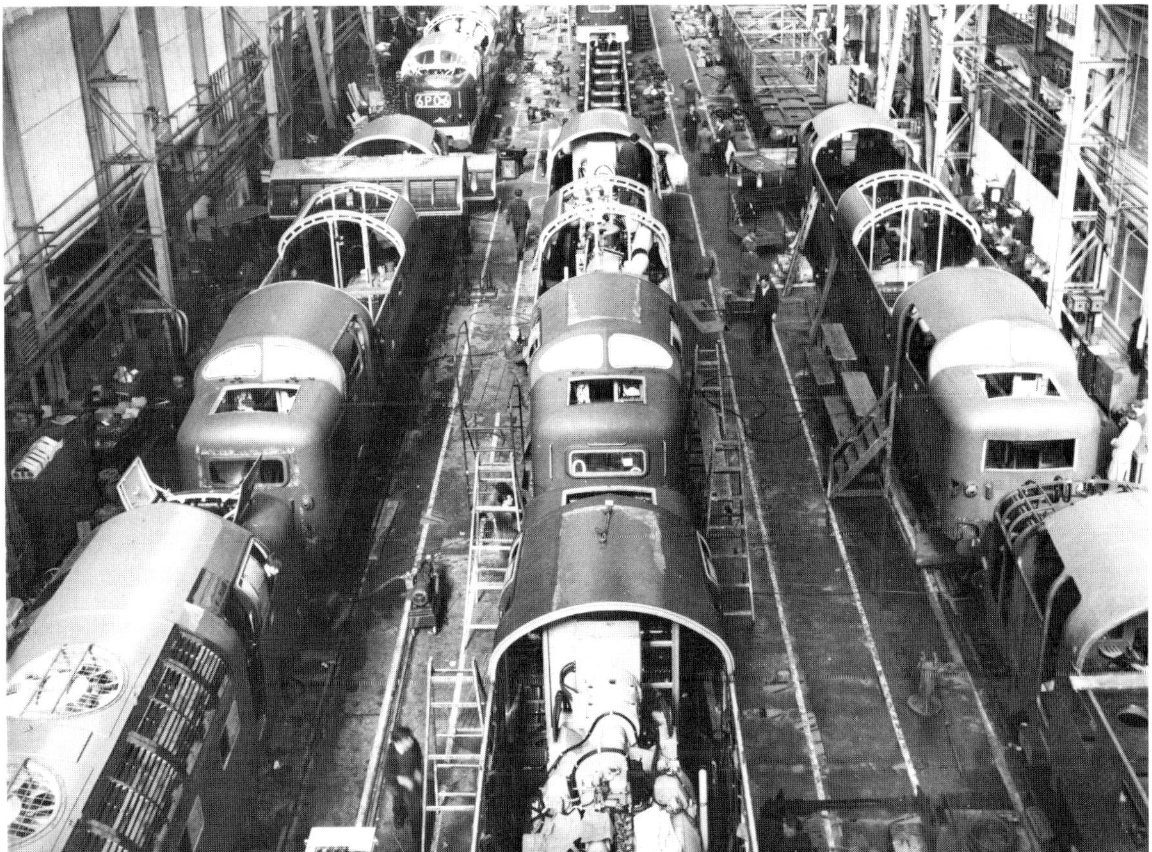
6P06

Above: The Birmingham RC&W Type 2, No D5344 at St Rollox in 1960./*G.W. Morrison*

Right: The Western Region's Type 4 'Western' class built in quantity but without prototypes. /*Sam Lambert*

Above: Railcars at work. A Swindon-built 'Trans-Pennine' unit on a Liverpool-York train near Mossley in 1977./*David A. Flitcroft*

Left: Business end of the first BR/Sulzer 2,300hp 1Co-Co1 No D1 *Scafell Pike.* /*Sam Lambert*

D 1

BRITISH RAILWAYS

Top: The 1961 motive power exhibition at Marylebone Goods showing four types of motive power: WR 'Hymek' diesel-hydraulic; the gas turbine GT3; a 25kV ac electric locomotive and one of SR 3-rail dc locomotives./*BR*

Not of significant interest in the development of major modernisation plan orders, but certainly eye-catching, were the now deceased diesel-electric Pullmans of 1960. Power car of the LMR's 'Midland Pullman' *(above)* near Duffield in March 1960, when on test. WR 8-car set *(left)* at Paddington in 1964.
/*Both: Sam Lambert*

By 1959 dieselisation was already changing the face of some BR main lines. A BRCW Type 2 *(above right)*, more usually associated with Scotland, near Woolmer Green on an up Cambridge 'slow'. Cravens-built 2-car sets *(right)* making up a GN main line stopping train, also near Woolmer Green.
/*E. R. Wethersett; Ian Allan Library*

5
Aspects of Transition

When the Railway Executive was abolished the only member of it to join the British Transport Commission was J. C. L. (later Sir Landale) Train, and he became the Engineering member. On the Railway Executive he had been the Member for Civil, Signal, and Telecommunications Engineering, and had previously been Chief Civil Engineer of the London & North Eastern Railway. J. Ratter, who had been Technical Adviser on the General Staff, succeeded Train, when he retired, and was himself succeeded on the General Staff by Bond. Until Bond joined the General Staff, therefore, neither the Engineering member on the Commission nor the Technical Adviser had been either a Mechanical or an Electrical Engineer.

The four Chief Engineers of the British Railways Central Staff worked under the general supervision of the Technical Adviser and reported to him; thus when Bond became Technical Adviser his overall responsibility included those matters which came under Harrison and Warder. Bond's principal duties were to co-ordinate technical opinion for submission to the Commission, and to guide technical development and practices.[1] He did not interfere with matters which he regarded as being within the competence of the CME. A minor aspect of locomotive design illustrates this. Bond insisted on all the larger locomotives designed while he was CME having 'nose' ends, because he thought that they gave some protection, countered 'sleeper flicker', and gave the locomotives a better appearance. Harrison, when he became CME, had all locomotives built with flat ends; firstly because he liked them that way, and secondly because he considered the nose only useful to use up space on a 1Co-Co1 locomotive. Bond thought that it would be improper for him to interfere with this decision. On the other hand, Bond was not satisfied with the 'Hymeks' and he asked Harrison to see that all future orders for Type 3s were confined to the English Electric locomotives. However, there was no difference of opinion on the merits of the 'Hymeks', for Harrison did not like them either![2]

There was yet another reorganisation as a result of the Transport Act of 1962. The Transport Commission was abolished and separate Boards were established for the various transport activities. Sir Brian Robertson retired in June 1961 and Dr Richard Beeching became Chairman of the Railway Board, the members of which were given functional responsibilities very similar to those exercised by the members of the Railway Executive. The General Staff disappeared, and the four Chief Engineers reported direct to the Board Member. However, Bond was kept on as Technical Adviser, because there were many technical matters concerning more than one department which still needed attention. Part of the reorganisation was the grouping of the main railway workshops into a Workshops Division, to which Bond was appointed Technical Adviser. On 1 January 1965, he succeeded Owen Houchen as General Manager.[3]

Warder retired after the institution of the new regime and the posts of CME and CEE were combined under Harrison, whose designation was now Chief Engineer (Traction and Rolling Stock), a title borrowed from the French Railways' *Ingenieur en Chef du Materiel et de la Traction.*[4] This somewhat cumbersome terminology was retained until after the appointment of T. C. B. Miller in 1968. The title of CME was then, to Miller's joy, restored, but without any change in responsibilities.[5]

Before Bond vacated his position as CME, there had been an interesting excursion into the possibilities of gas turbines to provide motive power. As already stated, the Great Western's trials of gas turbine locomotives had not been very successful, but sufficient experience had been gained to warrant further experiment. British Railways therefore became associated with a project, sponsored by the Ministry of Fuel and Power between 1951 and 1959, for a gas turbine burning pulverised coal. The North British Locomotive Company were to build the locomotive and C. A. Parsons were to supply a 1,750hp gas turbine. However, because of difficulties on test in the works, the locomotive was never completed. A Parliamentary Question in March 1979 elicited the reply that information about the cost of this programme 'is no longer available'.[6] A project by the English Electric Company was much more promising, for they built at the Vulcan Foundry a gas turbine locomotive, known as GT3, which ran some thousands of miles on the main lines. The engineer in charge of the project, John Hughes, had found Bond's paper on the LMS steam turbine locomotive, No 6202, of considerable help in the design. Hughes consulted Bond on many aspects of the locomotive, and particularly as to whether it should be carried on two bogies, or have a rigid wheelbase and main frames like a steam locomotive. Bond opted for the latter to avoid a duplex drive to each of the bogies, with the complications of cardan shafts and bevel drives on a number of axles. The locomotive was accordingly built as a 4-6-0, with a separate corridor tender carrying fuel and a train heating boiler. It had a singularly close resemblance to a streamlined steam locomotive with inside cylinders. GT3 worked special passenger trains at express timings over the London Midland Region main lines, and on one of the test trips Bond rode on the footplate and drove it. He says that it was a splendid locomotive and did very well on its trial runs, but some further development was needed to ensure that it was sufficiently reliable. Unfortunately money was not available and a promising project had to be abandoned.

J. F. Harrison, when he took over as CME, did not view the diesel scene with any enthusiasm. He was confronted with a few locomotives of 10 different types, the forerunners of the 174, with lots more untried classes on order. He says that by the time he arrived as CME in October 1958, the trial period had been abandoned and the damage done:

'It left a situation which I had to rectify by selecting what I thought were the best types, and the more difficult task of trying to get rid of the unsatisfactory ones. In this latter case great pressures were put upon the Board by private firms, whose locomotives were unsatisfactory, to be given another chance. This made life difficult as you can imagine, and when it came to battling with the Western Region, well nigh impossible. Eventually, years later, the Western realised their mistake (not technical) and ran many trains with diesel-electrics ... It wasn't until 1959 that diesel-hydraulic purchases ceased, although 1,700hp "Hymeks" and 2,700hp Maybach/Voith were ordered and built in quantity without prototypes. It is interesting to note that after extensive testing by Western Region of the Mekydro transmission that these mechanical transmissions did not appear in the 2,700hp Maybach/Voith. The cause of the Mekydro transmission failures was the effect of reverse torques when operating freight trains.'[7]

The heavy Type 4 1Co-Co1 diesel-electric locomotives came in for some criticisim. In June 1961 *Diesel Railway Traction* said:

'For some time it has been known that a design had been developed to replace for new construction those cumbersome 1Co-Co1 locomotives of 2,300/2,500bhp of 140 tons weight by a Co-Co unit of weight and proportions a little more in accordance with sound ideas; but the first public reference to this was made at the recent modernisation conference in London, when Mr J. F. Harrison spoke of a weight of 114 tons for these coming locomotives ... Even so, 114 tons is far more than should be necessary for that purpose [ie greater braking power for unbraked goods trains], and a service weight of 100/102 tons on a Co-Co axle arrangement can be considered a generous allowance for a diesel electric locomotive.'

At that time *Diesel Railway Traction* was looking favourably at the light locomotive weight that could be achieved by using the high-speed German engines, combined with hydraulic or hydro-mechanical transmission. Harrison in the same month replied to such criticisms as follows:

'Type 4 locomotives of two designs were developed with the 1Co-Co1 axle arrangement at a weight of 130/140 tons. This was not a mistake but the only way at the time of combining available slow-speed engines, train heating,

and 18.5 tons axle loading. Besides being uneconomically heavy, these locomotives will not traverse vertical humps in marshalling yards, so that their full usage in mixed traffic working is limited ... It is difficult for boilers so restricted in available room to become fully reliable. It had accordingly been decided to dual-fit main line carriage stock with electric heating provided by an auxiliary heating generator driven from the main engine ... Experience in service has shown that no clear choice between high-speed or medium-speed engines, or between electric and hydraulic transmissions has yet emerged.'

This last sentence was of course true, but Harrison did not think that high-speed engines provided the correct solution. He wrote to the Author:

'I do not like high speed engines. The argument was always that one could design a locomotive of given horsepower with less weight by using them. I found they were much more unreliable than medium-speed engines, and although one might reduce the weight of the locomotive overall, this was not necessarily an advantage as adhesion was also reduced, with consequent slipping at starting.'[8]

The argument between the protagonists of the high-speed diesel engine with hydraulic transmission and those who favoured medium-speed engines with electric transmission was ultimately put to the test in 1965, and the results were given in the *Report on Diesel-Electric and Diesel-Hydraulic Locomotives on British Railways*, which was issued by the Department of the Chief Engineer (Traction and Rolling Stock) in August 1965.

Four classes of locomotives, two with each of the two forms of transmission and each of a pair being comparable, were selected for more detailed analysis; and running trials were carried out with one of these pairs – a 'Western' class diesel-hydraulic and a Brush/Sulzer diesel-electric, both of about 2,700hp. Comparisons were made of performance, first cost, efficiency, availability, casualty rate, and the nature of defects. It was not possible, however, to compare maintenance costs because neither of the two classes concerned had yet achieved complete repair cycles.

The report found that both diesel-electric and diesel-hydraulic locomotives were capable of running the railway, but that operating availability and reliability differed. An attempt had been made to find out which of the adverse features of each class were due to design and manufacturing defects, and which were inherent features of the two transmission systems.

At the time of the report there were in service on British Railways 2,315 main line diesel-electric locomotives and 358 main line diesel-hydraulic locomotives, and of these substantial numbers in different groups with electric transmission had their direct counterparts with hydraulic transmission. In consequence, British Railways had probably greater comparative experience of these two basic varieties of diesel locomotive practice than the railways of any other country.

In the beginning, and particularly in the 2,000hp range,

the diesel-hydraulic had a marked advantage in the power-to-weight ratio, because the 2,200hp Maybach/Mekydro diesel-hydraulic locomotive had a weight of only 80 tons and four axles; whereas the English Electric 2,000hp diesel-electric locomotive had eight axles and weighed 133 tons. (Strictly speaking the Mekydro transmission is, of course, hydro-mechanical and not hydraulic). Since those early days, however, it had been established that engine power of the order of 2,700hp was required for the heavier passenger and freight duties throughout British Railways. Within the, by this time, universally permitted axle load on main lines of 19 tons, this called for six axles, whether the locomotive had an electric or a hydraulic transmission. Under these circumstances, said the report, the ratio of engine power to total weight was much closer; the inherent lighter weight of high-speed engines and hydraulic transmission being counterbalanced by the need to use two engines as against one in the case of electric transmission with medium-speed engines. However, at this stage of the argument the report is muddling two separate issues: high-speed versus medium-speed engines, and hydraulic versus electric transmission; for neither type of engine is tied to either type of transmission. For instance, both the 'Deltic' locomotive and the High Speed Train have high-speed engines and electric transmission. Indeed, the North British Locomotive Company had built two classes of Type 2 locomotives with high-speed engines which were practically identical, except that one class had electric transmission and the other hydraulic; but the former weighed 73 tons and the latter 65.

Comprehensive tests were carried out under controlled road conditions by the Swindon Experimental Unit on the 2,750hp diesel-electric D1500 (later 47) class and the 2,700hp diesel-hydraulic D1000 or 'Western' (later 52) class.

In tractive effort D1500 produced 71,700lb at 6.5 mile/h as against D1000's 65,900 at 4mile/h, both under normal rail conditions. D1000 was the more sure-footed, because isolated wheel slip could be checked more readily by torque transfer through the cardan shaft, ie because the wheels were coupled.

On D1500 rail maximum hp was maintained practically constant at 2,250hp between 30mile/h and 80mile/h. On D1000 the physical connection between the road wheels and the engines caused the power demand to be dependent upon the ratio of the input to the output speed. The maximum engine speed of 1,500 rev/min was only reached at 55mile/h. Owing to the characteristics of hydraulic transmission the rail hp remained in the region of 2,000 for much of the speed range.

The comparison between the two as regards continuous and short-period rating was extremely interesting. The report points out that ideally any locomotive should be capable of maintaining continuously throughout the speed range any tractive effort that it is capable of exerting. Because the locomotives covered by the report were general purpose, they had to (a) give the specified performance at maximum speed, (b) start heavy trains and under adverse conditions, and (c) continue working for

appreciable periods at the maximum tractive effort that adhesion would permit.

Electric transmission can only provide universal continuous rating if the traction motors are large and heavy in relation to output, in order to limit the temperature rise, or alternatively are associated with change-speed gearing. If axle load or price imposes a limit, then a choice has to be made in the traction motor and gear design in favour of either the low speed or the high speed parts of a locomotive's duty. D1500 had to be at its best at the highest speeds, so that, within a 19ton axle load, the transmission was so proportioned that the maximum speed of continuous working at full power was declared by the makers at the rather high rate of 27mile/h, with a tractive effort of 30,000lb and an overall transmission efficiency of 83%. The one-hour rating was 23.3mile/h and 34,300lb tractive effort at 81% transmission efficiency. This, however, fell far short of the effort that adhesion would permit, so a ten-minute rating was introduced for certain freight duties. This allowed 41,500lb tractive effort at 17.5mile/h, with 77% transmission efficiency.

Different considerations applied to the English Electric Type 3, the 1,750hp D6700; for this class was primarily employed on freight working and the requirements at maximum speed were therefore less exacting. It was designed, therefore, for a continuous tractive effort of 35,000lb at 13.6mile/h, with a transmission efficiency of 79%.

Hydraulic transmission incorporates gear change stages, and therefore continuous or short term ratings as factors do not really apply. If the cooling needed is assured by choosing the required external radiator capacity, the maximum tractive effort can be held for appreciable periods at stall point without harming the transmission. D1000 could operate at a continuous rating under full power at 14.5mile/h. On test the temperature of the transmission oil remained at an acceptable level during full power working at 13mile/h, when the tractive effort was 45,800lb. Transmission efficiency was then only 63%, but the cooling system was able to cope indefinitely with the 35% rejected as heat.

Under British conditions these differences in the characteristics of the two transmission systems were of negligible importance, but when long continuous gradients had to be climbed with heavy trains, as on some American lines, the hydraulic system could prove attractive.

On D1500 the efficiency between generator output and output at the rail varied from 83.5% to 84.25% at from 30 to 80mile/h. On D1000 the efficiency between 30 and 90mile/h was from 78% to 82%. The diesel-electric developed at rail 80.5% to 81.5% of the maximum installed engine power, whilst the figures for the diesel hydraulic were 74%-77%.

The specific fuel consumption of the locomotives in lb/rail hp/hr was lower for D1500 by some 4% to 6% over the range of train speed.

As regards costs, D1500 cost £125,000 and D1000 £136,000; whilst the D6700 (later class 37) Type 3 diesel-electric cost £83,250 as compared with the £87,950 for D7000 'Hymek' (later Class 35).

Both classes of diesel-electric locomotives had better availability than the two diesel-hydraulics. The averages over 10 4-weekly periods in 1964 were: D1500, 86.1%; D1000, 64.3%; D6700, 90.5%; and D7000, 82.8%.

On British Railways a casualty is defined as: 'Any defect or occurrence to a locomotive in traffic which prevents it from completing the working of its booked train, or causes loss of time or a late start to the extent of five minutes or more in passenger working, or ten minutes or more in freight working.' Casualties for any given class of locomotive are also related to its load factor, that is, the percentage of total work done to total time. D1500 and D1000 could therefore be compared because their duties were similar, as could also D6700 and D7000. In the whole life of these locomotives up till the time of the tests the miles per casualty figures for the diesel-electrics were much better than those for the diesel-hydraulics. They were as follows: (a) D1500, 11,000; D1000, 8,500; (b) D6700, 31,000; and D7000, 18,000. Transmission casualties alone were over four times as high per locomotive for hydraulic as for electric, but all transmission casualties together represented only 12% of all casualties.

In the light of the above and other factors, the report concluded that: 'From their own experience British Railways consider that the balance of advantage is now,

and will remain, in favour of electric transmission under their particular operating conditions. They have decided that all current and future orders are or will be diesel electric.'

Later, when maintenance costs could be compared, the diesel-hydraulics were found very expensive to maintain. Furthermore maintenance eventually became difficult because the North British Locomotive Company went out of business and all spares had to be obtained from Germany, with delays of sometimes up to nine months.[9]

Notes

1 Bond Roland C.; *A Lifetime with Locomotives;* Cambridge, Goose & Son, 1975, p220
2 Bond, R. C.; Information to the Author, Harrison, J. F.; Information to the Author
3 Bond; *A Lifetime with Locomotives,* op cit, pp277-8, 282, 298
4 Bond, Information to the Author
5 ibid, *A Lifetime with Locomotives,* pp261-2
6 PQ from Mr Robert Adley, MP, to Secretary of State for Energy, 27 March 1979
7 Harrison, J. F.; Letter to the Author
8 ibid
9 Miller, T. C. B.; Information to the Author.

Below: Outline drawing of North British coal burning gas turbine locomotive.

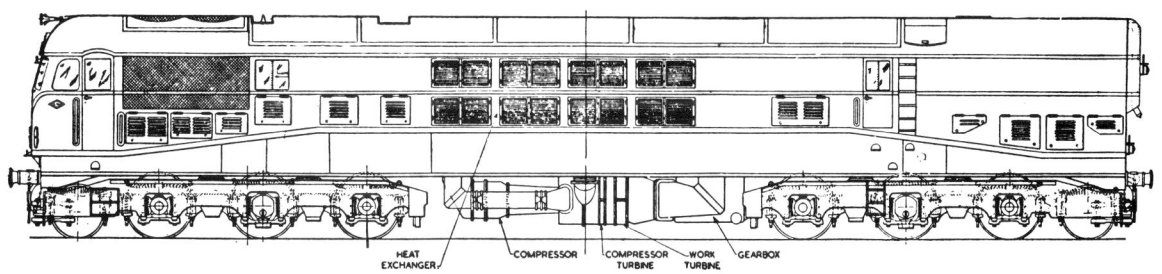

HEAT EXCHANGER — COMPRESSOR — COMPRESSOR TURBINE — WORK TURBINE — GEARBOX

Above: The reality of transition: steam and diesel being stabled together at Holbeck depot in April 1966./*L.A. Nixon*

Centre left: English Electric's gas turbine locomotive, No GT3, at Leicester GC shed in 1961./*E. Rawstron*

Below left: A Western Region Hymek, No D7057, at Paddington in February 1963 when deliveries of this class were progressing fast /*Sam Lambert*

Above right: Line-up of Brush Type 4s, now Class 47, at Knottingley Depot in 1971; these were being used on merry-go-round coal trains. /*N.E. Preedy*

Right: One of the 'cumbersome' 1Co-Co1 Type 4 diesel-electrics, No D2, which was actually fleet of foot enough to come up from Liverpool to Euston in 161min in June 1964, a precursor of 'electric' standards of running. The record breaking special on arrival at Euston. /*M.S. Welch*

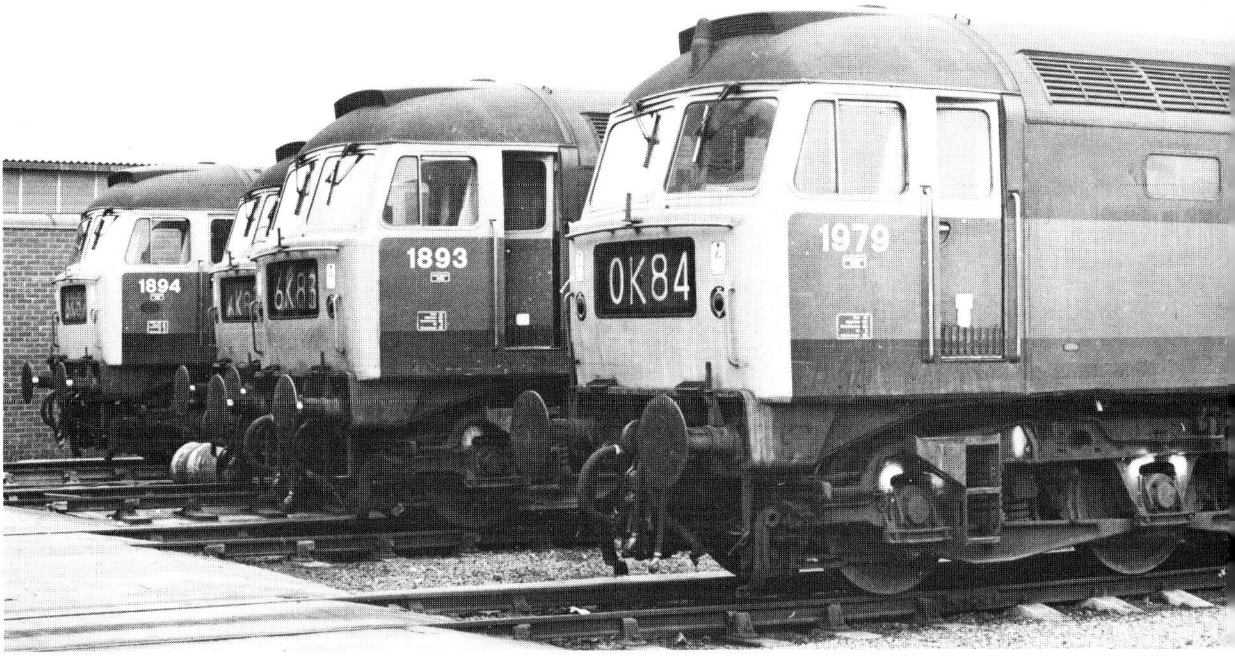
1894
1893
1979
6K83
0K84

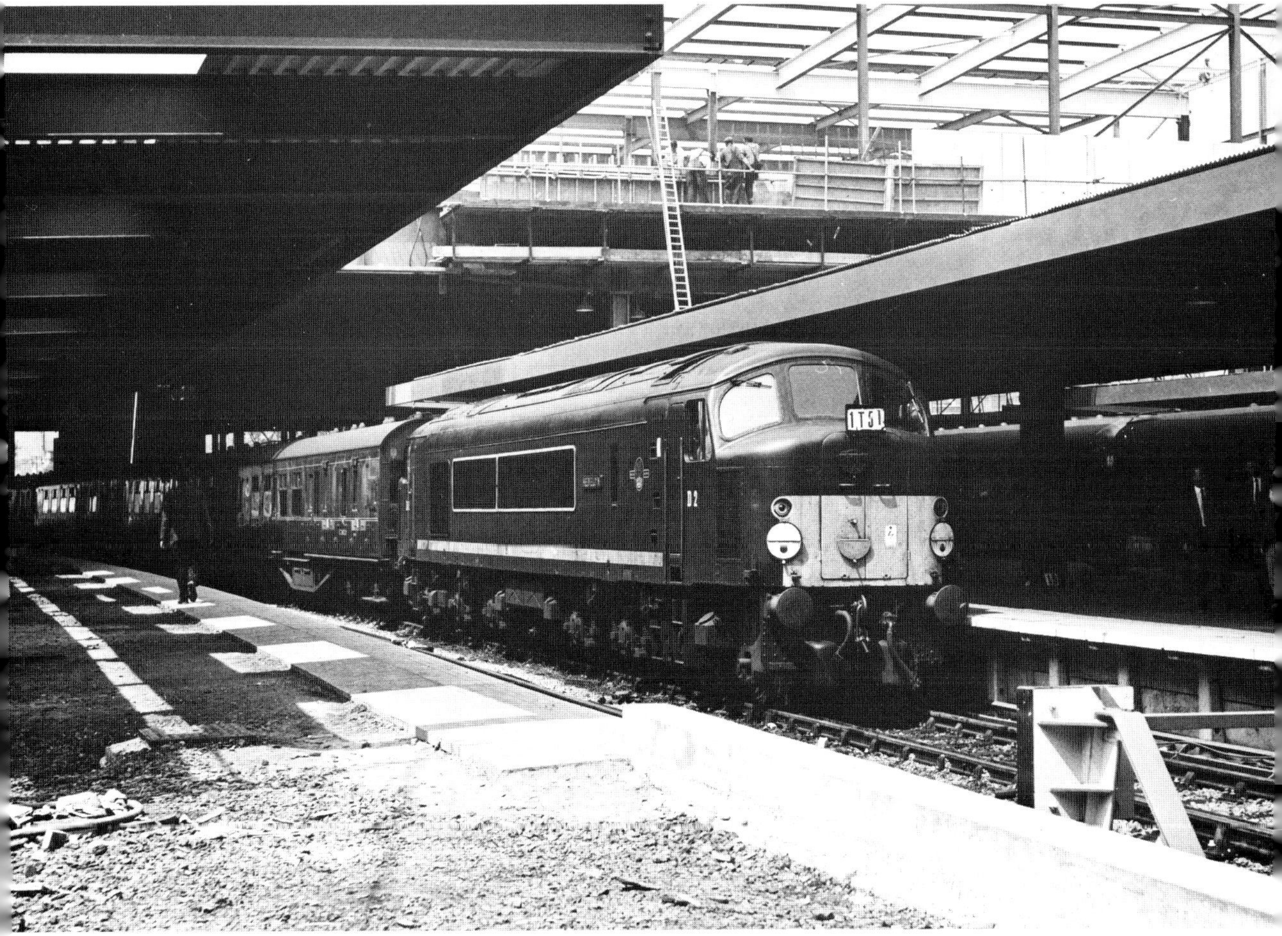
1T51
D2

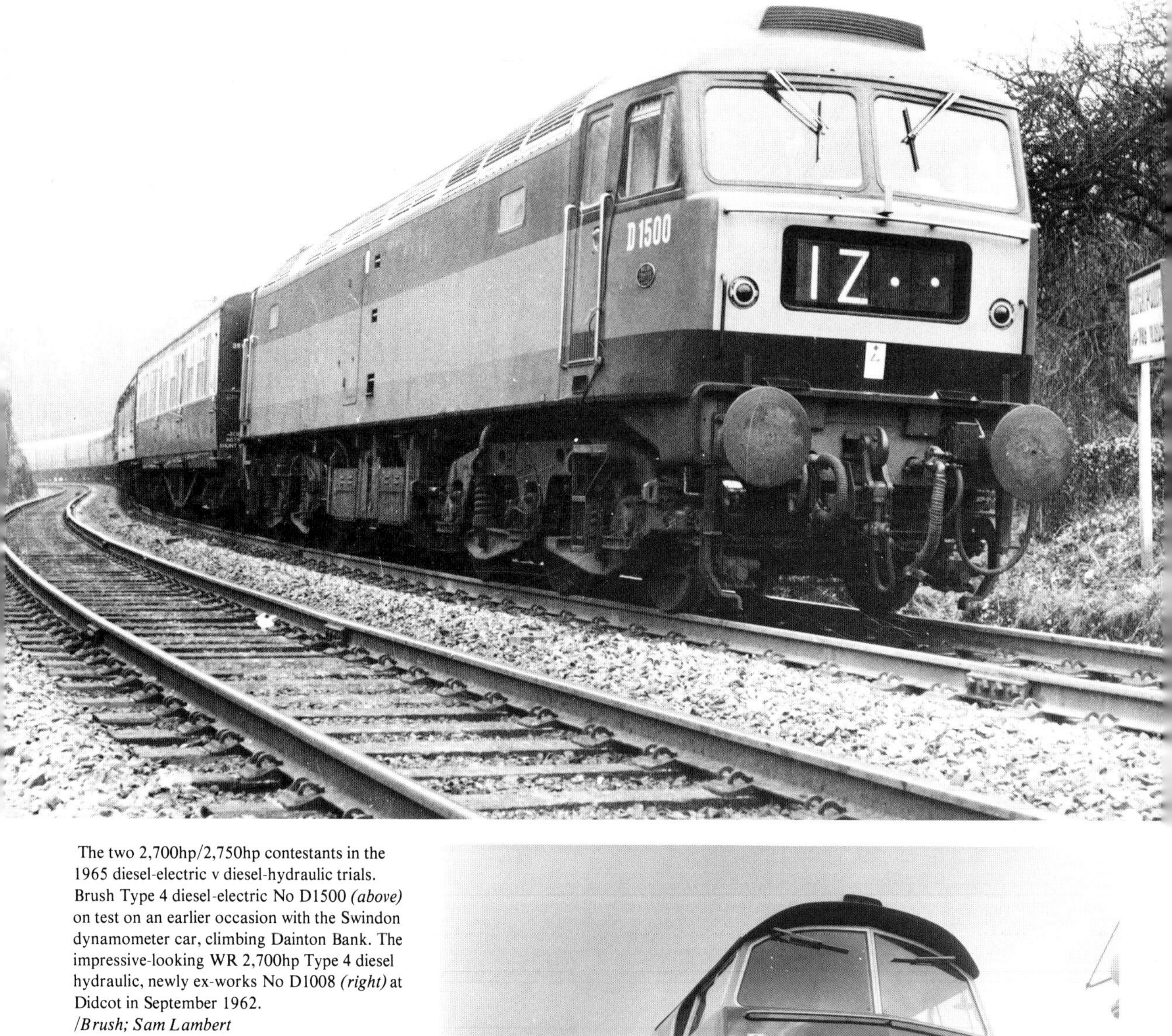

The two 2,700hp/2,750hp contestants in the
1965 diesel-electric v diesel-hydraulic trials.
Brush Type 4 diesel-electric No D1500 *(above)*
on test on an earlier occasion with the Swindon
dynamometer car, climbing Dainton Bank. The
impressive-looking WR 2,700hp Type 4 diesel
hydraulic, newly ex-works No D1008 *(right)* at
Didcot in September 1962.
/Brush; Sam Lambert

Top: New Brush Type 4, No D1504, attracts attention at Finsbury Park station, in January 1963./*Sam Lambert*

Above: The English Electric capability – a 1965 press photograph showing current orders from Vulcan Works for BR, and one of the Company's 0-4-0 diesel shunters. Left to right. SR electro diesel, 25kV Class AL6 electric locomotive, Type 1 Bo-Bo diesel-electric, Type 3 Co-Co diesel-electric./*GEC*

Left: A Sulzer 12LDA28-C diesel engine with the generator coupled to it is lowered into position in a Brush Type 4 at the manufacturer's Loughborough plant./*Brush*

Above: Through the 1960s diesels had progressively replaced steam on all shunting and pilot jobs. Two 350hp diesel-electric shunters, by now Class 08, work an afternoon trip to Manvers Main Colliery out of Wath Yard in October 1978./*Rev Graham B. Wise*

Centre right: The current scene: A Bedwyn-Reading dmu (with a very odd destination shown!) passes Colthrop, on the Berks & Hants line, in 1979 as a Class 47 waits for its oil tank train to be discharged./*D.E. Canning*

Below right: Steam at the beginning of the chapter, and at the end. Much management effort was spent in the organisational aspects of the steam to diesel changeover; worse still, works had to be closed. This is the doomed Gorton Works in 1963, with the last steam locomotive to receive major repairs there being hauled out by a diesel shunter./*BR*

6
Steam Departure

The previous four chapters have been devoted to diesel power, but it is important to remember that steam locomotives were working trains on British Railways up till 1968, and, as Bond points out, improvements in the smokebox and draughting continued right up till the end. Timings of trains were getting back to prewar standards with steam power, and on the Western Region this was due largely to improvements made to the 'Kings' and 'Castles' in extra superheat and better draughting.[1] On the Eastern Region performance and economy in coal consumption were vastly improved by the fitting of Kylchap double exhausts to the A4 and A3 Pacifics. The latter were once again handling the main line expresses from Kings Cross to Newcastle and Leeds. The resulting softer exhaust on the A3s led to smoke and steam obscuring the driver's vision, but this was cured by fitting German type smoke deflectors. In addition six V2 2-6-2s were provided with double Kylchaps because a standing pilot had to be kept at Peterborough to cover any diesels which failed, particularly 'Deltics', and the Peterborough turntable would not take any engine longer than a V2. The results were so outstanding that one of the enginemen's representatives at New England said that it was not diesels they wanted but Kylchap double blastpipes.[2] In addition to these older engines there were, of course, the fine modern steam locomotives designed by Riddles, and of these the 'Britannias' achieved fame in their punctual running of the two-hour and hourly 'Broadsman' expresses on the Great Eastern line. The average consumption of coal and water showed the skill with which the engines were driven on this exacting schedule; but the figures also supported Riddles' contention that theoretical improvement in thermal efficiency may be quite meaningless because different practices in driving and firing will lead to widely different results with the same engine. Of the average rates of consumption per journey by the 'Britannias' with nine different crews, the lowest was 2,448gal of water and 3,060lb of coal, and the highest 3,077gal water and 3,846lb of coal. The intermediate figures were spread fairly evenly between them.[3]

Following the good results obtained with Caprotti poppet valve gear on 4-6-2 No 71000, *Duke of Gloucester,* these valves were fitted to a number of Class 5 4-6-0s, with consequent lower maintenance costs, and a reduction in coal consumption of from 5 to 10%. In performance the Caprotti engines were about equal to those fitted with Walschaerts valve gear. A plain double blastpipe was tried on some 4-6-0s for a comparison with engines of the same classes having a single blastpipe. There was no difference. Crosti boilers were tried on some

2-10-0s, in a search for greater efficiency, but they were a failure; and a Giesl ejector tried on one of the same class did nothing to improve these very efficient engines. Bond fitted mechanical stokers to three 2-10-0s to exploit the maximum capacity of the boilers and so enable them to haul heavy freight trains at speed. The experiment was successful, but unfortunately the operating people could not provide these engines with sufficient jobs to make use of their increased capacity.[4]

On some of the foreign railways that were transferring to diesel traction, the proper maintenance of steam locomotives was allowed to lapse. On British Railways, on the contrary, there was constant effort to get more miles between repairs and higher mileages per annum.[5]

One of the most remarkable steam events of this period was the rebuilding of the Southern Railway Bulleid Pacifics between 1955 and 1961. Owing to the expensive maintenance and heavy coal consumption of these controversial locomotives, Riddles gave instructions that they were to be rebuilt on more conventional lines.[6] Riddles had retired before the rebuilding began, and it was carried out under the general direction of R. C. Bond, who was now CME BTC, and under the immediate supervision of H. H. Swift, CM&EE Southern Region. The detailed design, however, was carried out at Brighton by R. G. Jarvis, Chief Technical Assistant (Locomotives), who had come from the LMS. In a letter to the author he wrote that rebuilding was necessary because of the unreliability, high maintenance cost, and heavy coal and oil consumption arising from the several revolutionary features of the engines in their original condition; and in fact the cost of the rebuilding was recovered in four years.

It was first thought that it would be impossible to rebuild them in the more traditional form with Walschaerts valve gear; however this problem was solved. Jarvis continues:

'We had to give a good deal of thought to the most economical way of eliminating the troublesome features whilst retaining other features, such as the boiler and chassis, which were in most respects excellent. The basic scheme was to dispense with the chain-driven valve gear and oil bath and the "air-smooth" casing. We used BR standard parts wherever possible, but did not replace any more than was strictly necessary to effect the desired improvements in performance and reliability.

'It was found possible to retain the outside cylinders by adapting a fairly standard Walschaerts gear to outside admission and using new steamchest covers with United Kingdom cast iron packings, which had already been used very successfully on the Southern Region. Actually, the valve gear was based on that for the BR 2-6-4 tank locomotives, which were also designed at Brighton.

'For the inside cylinder a new steel casting was provided, as the steamchest had to be moved over from the centre line of the cylinder to the right hand side, so as to be in line with the Walschaerts valve gear. As this was a completely new inside "engine", standard practice was followed using inside admission. This at least made high pressure valve spindle packings unnecessary, where they would have been more difficult of access.'

I had expressed surprise that it had been found possible to use Walschaerts valve gear for an inside cylinder driving on the middle coupled axle, because I had understood that the difficulty of clearance over the leading axle had been one of the reasons for Gresley's derived gear and Bulleid's chain drive. However, Jarvis answered this as follows:

The Walschaerts valve gear was very straightforward and did not present us with any especially difficult problems. Possibly head-room was available because the tapering of the boiler was on the underside, sloping upwards to the smokebox and it was virtually horizontal at the top (ie the reverse of Churchward's taper boilers).

'The only unusual feature was the attachment of the single eccentric to the RH crank sweep by means of a spigot and five studs. This modification was also applied to the unrebuilt engines, for the attachment of the chain-driven sprocket; the original clamped-on fitting having been a factor in axle fatigue failure. When this modification was introduced the plans for rebuilding were well advanced, and the opportunity was taken to prepare the crank axles beforehand to receive their eccentrics. This also ensured that the pairs of driving wheels were reasonably interchangeable between rebuilt and unrebuilt locomotives. (The outside crankpins, however, were not standard.)

'I suppose that locomotives with three cylinders, all driving on the second pair of coupled wheels, and having three independent sets of Walschaerts valve gear are rare, but Stanier's 3-cylinder 2-6-4 tank for the Tilbury section is a precedent.

'I would imagine that Gresley's main object in using a derived gear was to eliminate the eccentric. I would not think that divided drive was adopted because of any special difficulty with the inside valve gear. Tests have shown that any derived or indirect drive to piston valves is less efficient than the direct attachment of the valve gear to the valve spindle. This even applied to GWR 4-cylinder designs with their rocking levers.

'Certainly the rebuilt Bulleid Pacifics behaved very well, and Sam Ell, who conducted the tests of No 35020, told me that they were the most predictable engines he had ever tested (praise indeed from Swindon). I am afraid that Mr Bulleid never quite forgave me.'

As regards the LMS 3-cylinder tank engines, Bond says that it was not possible to have a divided drive, as on other LMS 3-cylinder classes, because the leading pony truck did not allow sufficient room for an inside cylinder driving on the leading coupled axle.[7]

Bond says that the rebuilding turned an engine which was very expensive to use and maintain into one of the best. Indeed the rebuilt 'Merchant Navies' were, he considers, comparable to the LMS 'Duchesses'.[8] This was a considerable compliment because Bond has always considered the latter to have been the best of British Class 8 Pacifics.

The rebuilt Southern Pacifics had the distinction of working the last main line steam hauled expresses. Having regard to the rapid advance of Southern electrification, there can have been few in earlier years who would have forecast that this would have happened on the old London & South Western. I saw one of the last of these trains arriving at Waterloo in 1967 behind a rebuilt 'Merchant Navy', and was astonished to see the letters SECR on the leading tender axlebox! So was the driver when I pointed it out to him. Jarvis, however, says that it was not so surprising as Ashford axleboxes had been standardised for the Southern Railway and this would have been merely an old cover.[9]

It had been planned to transfer some of the 'Duchesses' to the Southern Region, but trouble with clearances prevented this. These magnificent engines were therefore perforce withdrawn much earlier, and all had gone by the end of 1964. They maintained their high standard to the end, and Bond mentions a special run by No 6245 *City of London* from Glasgow to Euston which he considers equal to anything they had done in their earlier years. In Scotland unofficial trials were carried out on the night sleepers from Glasgow to compare 'Duchesses', Peppercorn A1s, and Gresley A4s, but there was nothing much to choose between them on these services.[10]

My own last memory of a 'Duchess' was at Euston in 1963. I was standing looking at the experimental diesel locomotive No DP2, which was about to leave on a down express, when I saw on the opposite platform a beautifully clean 'Duchess', resplendent in Midland red, backing slowly out after arriving on an up express. Another Euston end-of-steam memory is of a rebuilt 'Royal Scot', and of a crew full of enthusiasm for their engine and rather scornful of diesels.

Many of the top link drivers seemed to have shared this scorn for diesels. At Kings Cross I talked to the driver and fireman of A4 No 60017 (late 2512) *Silver Fox*, waiting to leave on a down express. They had just worked up on a 'Deltic' and were only too pleased to be back on a 'real' locomotive again. At Paddington, after arriving in a train hauled by an immaculate 'Castle', I asked the driver if he would rather be driving a diesel. He replied, 'Not while we have engines like these.' Pointing towards the managerial offices, he added, 'But the people up there are not interested in steam locomotives any more.'

Bond formed the opinion that the top link drivers did not like changing to diesel locomotives because they were skilled men with a pride in their craftsmanship, and little skill was needed to drive a diesel. He thought that most of the other drivers welcomed the change because they had a comfortable cab and could go home clean![11]

On the old LNER a few of the Peppercorn and Gresley Pacifics lasted till 1966; and of the very large classes of the useful B1 4-6-0s, quite a number were still running well into 1967. Thirteen of Riddles' outstanding 9F 2-10-0s lasted until the very end of steam in 1968.

The running down of steam without wasting money presented something of a problem. Locomotives at Kings Cross were scheduled to have a maintenance examination after 36,000 miles since overhaul. This was done in the running sheds, but T.C.B. Miller, when he was CM&EE Eastern Region, had it transferred to Doncaster. The tank engines were kept running by what became known as a 'half heel and sole' repair, till they were finally withdrawn, and the success of this system led to its being applied to the Pacifics as well. The latter, in fact, gave much better service as a result.[12]

The period when diesel was taking over from steam was roughly 1958 to 1968. In the former year the English Electric 2,000hp Type 4 (now Class 40) diesel-electric locomotives were entering traffic and working major main line express trains. Thenceforward the two types of motive power were working side by side, with the balance swinging gradually towards the diesel. There were many occasions when diesel failures led to steam locomotives making unexpected appearances on important trains, and there were occasionally steam revivals. In June 1961, for instance, it was decided that all the special trains from Kings Cross to York, on the occasion of the wedding of the Duke of Kent, should be worked by steam. All the beautifully turned out engines were Gresley A4s. No 60028 *Walter K. Whigham* hauled the Royal train carrying the Queen and the Royal family, and had the additional distinction of a white cab roof. Nos 60003 *Andrew K. McCosh* and 60015 *Quicksilver* worked the trains for the guests, and No 60014 *Silver Link* stood by as pilot. The General Manager watched the first of the trains steaming out from Kings Cross and remarked that even he could see that the locomotives were turned out in a condition of excellence that he could not achieve with the diesels.[13]

Notes

1 Bond, R. C.; Information to the Author
2 Townend, P. N.; *Top Shed;* Ian Allan, 1975, pp155-160
3 Colonel Rogers, H. C. B.; *The Last Steam Locomotive Engineer: R.A. Riddles, CBE;* London, George Allen & Unwin, 1970, p188
4 Bond, R. C.; op cit
5 ibid
6 Riddles, R. A.; Information to the Author
7 Bond, op cit
8 ibid
9 Jarvis, R. G.; Information to the Author
10 Bond, op cit,
11 ibid
12 Miller, T.C.B.; Information to the Author.
13 Townend, op cit, p172

Below: Postwar steam 'high noon'. Double chimneyed 'Castle' 4-6-0 No 7018 *Drysllwyn Castle* passes Swindon at high speed on the up 'Bristolian' in August 1956./*R.A. Panting*

Left: Steam departure: a newly outshopped 'Hall' 4-6-0 at Swindon Works in March 1959. WR allocated 'Britannia' (left) in for works attention./*Sam Lambert*

Below: 'Kylchaps' to the fore at Grantham shed, showing two A3s that had been modernised with double exhausts in the late 1950s/early 1960s with *Mallard* in between. She was one of the few A4s so equipped from the start./*Eric Oldham*

Right: One of the New England's stand-by double chimney V2s, No 60880, has been purloined for a Saturdays only Bournemouth-Newcastle train, seen on the GC main line in June 1962./*D. Holmes*

Below right: 'Britannia' finale. Very near the end of steam at Carlisle Kingmoor shed, 'Britannia' No 70013 accelerates a 13-coach Carlisle-Blackpool football special up past Wreay on Boxing Day, 1967./*Paul Claxton*

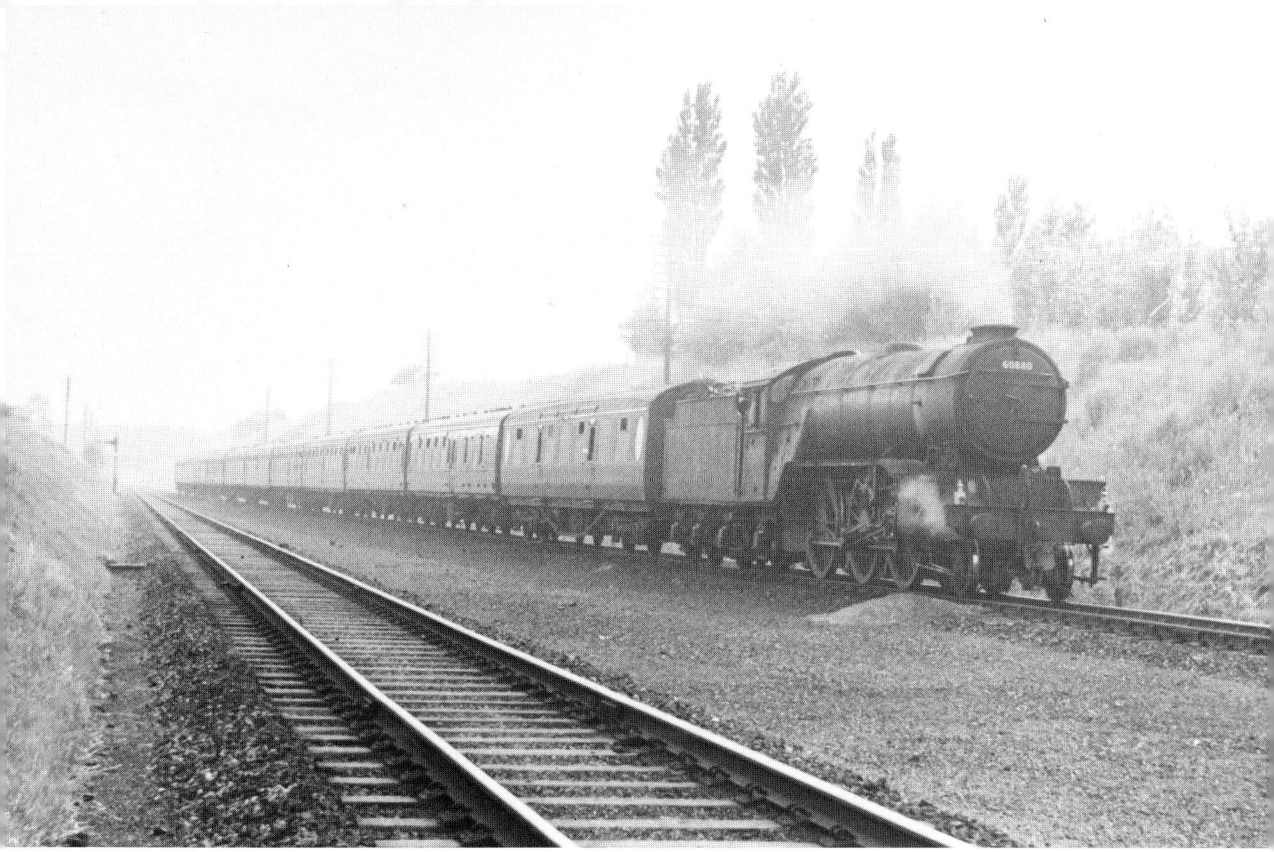

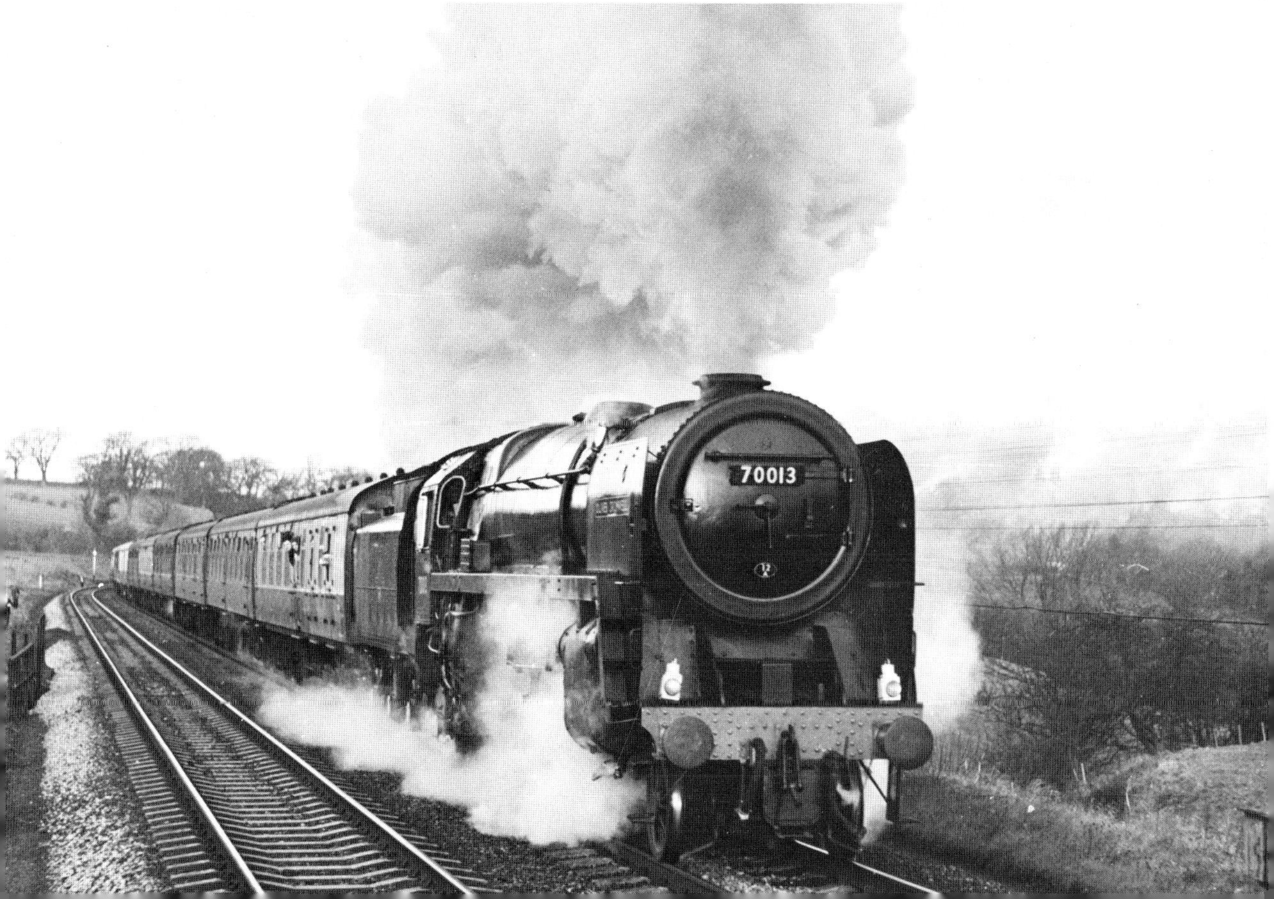
70013

A selection of departures from the basic BR Standard designs. *Top:* Caprotti-fitted '5' No 73148./*Brian E. Morrison. Above:* Double chimney '4' 4-6-0 No 75077./*P.J.C. Skelton. Top right:* Crosti in action, with smoke streaming from the righthand side 'chimney'. No 92026 on a Brent-Toton empties train near Mill Hill./*Brian E. Morrison. Centre right:* The Giesl ejector 9F reposes at Newport Ebbw Vale Junction shed in 1963./*A.J. Wheeler. Right:* A fine study of one of the stoker-fitted 9Fs, No 92167, between Hellifield and Skipton on an up express freight./*R.H. Short*

Top: The first 'Merchant Navy' to be rebuilt, No 35018 *British India Line,* at Eastleigh in 1956./*BR*

Above: One of the last Light Pacifics to be rebuilt, No 34101 *Hartland,* at Eastleigh in September 1960./*J. C. Haydon*

Top right: Into the setting sun, for Light Pacific No 34052 had not much longer to work when it hurried eastwards between Brockenhurst and Beaulieu Road on a Waterloo express in January 1967./*Ian S. Krause*

Centre right: Twilight of the 'Duchesses'. No 46235 *City of Birmingham* on Castlethorpe troughs with a Windermere-Euston express in late July 1964, only weeks before withdrawal./*R. L. Patrick*

Right: By February 1963, the date of this picture, the 'Castles' were on their way out and only the Paddington-Worcester trains were in their hands. No 5057 *Earl Waldegrave* takes the 11.15 down Worcester through Wolvercot Jn, Oxford./*G. Smith*

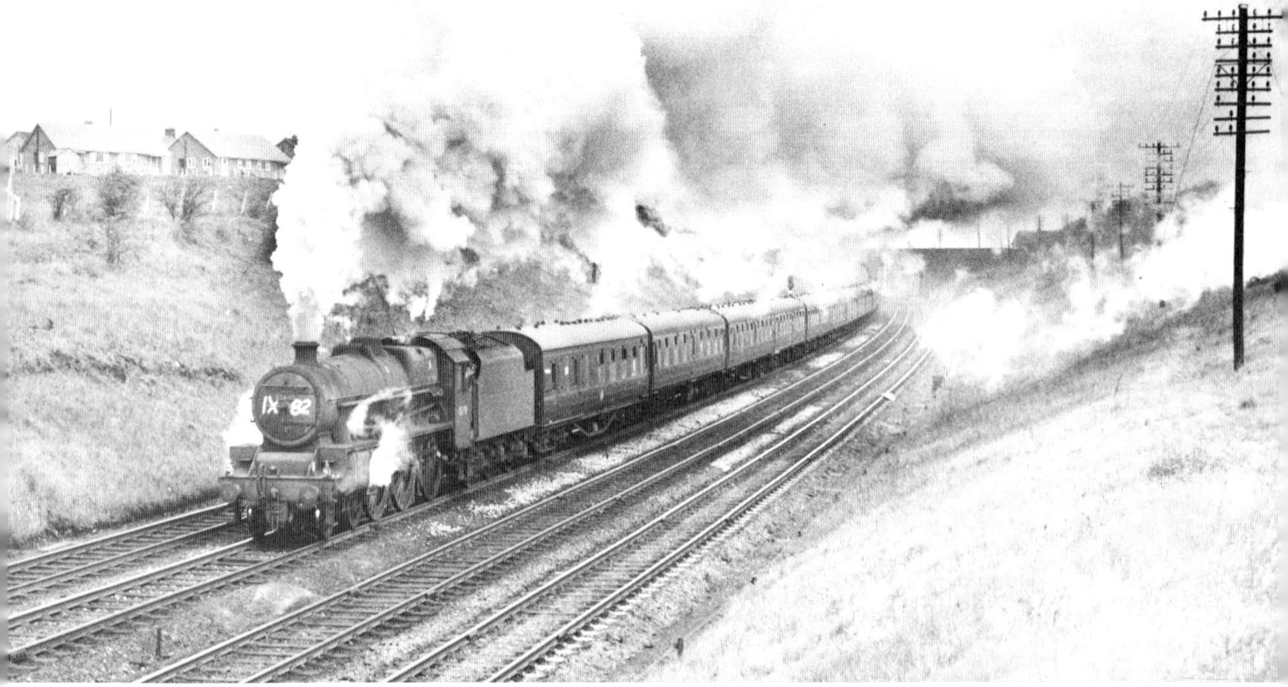
1X 82

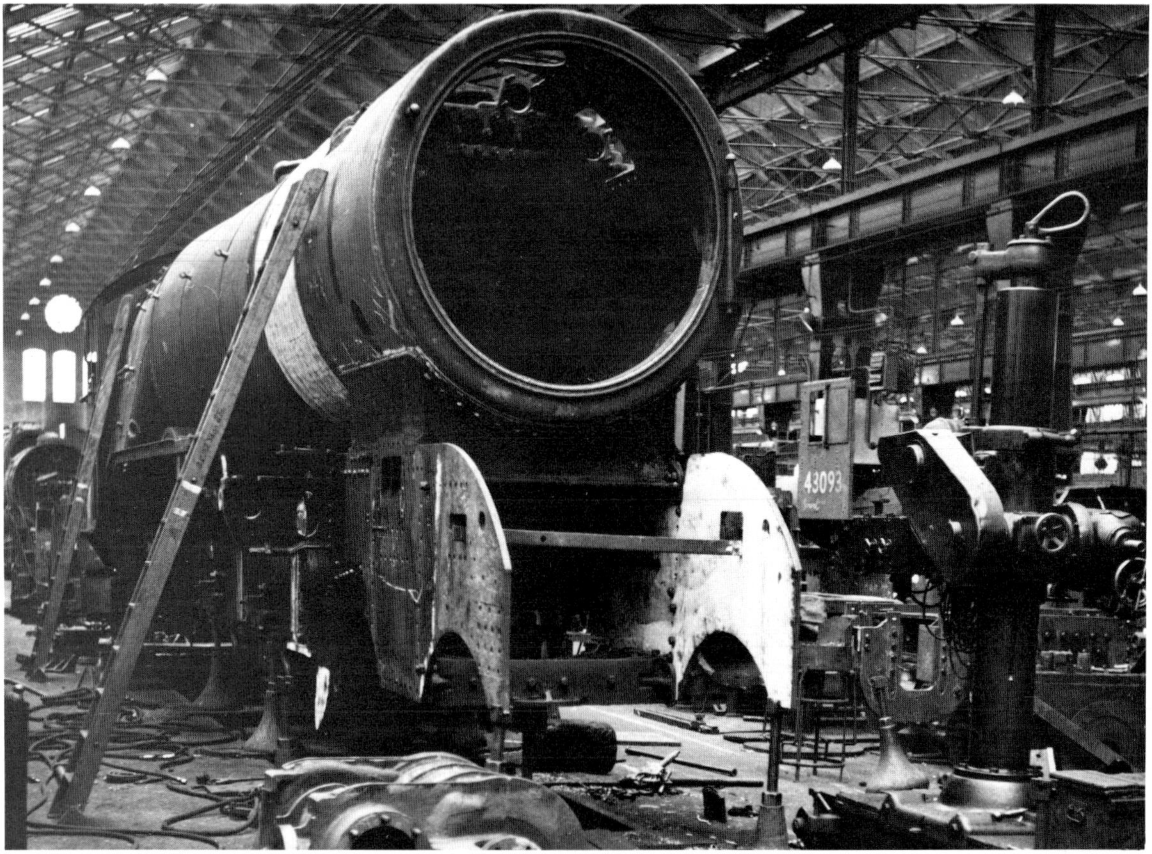
43093

Above left: An all-too common sight of the period, a filthy 'Jubilee' No 45693, leaking steam, struggles near Wigston North, Leicester on a football excursion in May 1963. Midland main line express trains were nearly all diesel by then./*G.D. King*

Left: A reminder of earlier steam repairs and the work they entailed is given by this shot of Darlington Works with Class A3 Pacific No 60074 receiving new three-quarters frames, (middle horn blocks to front buffer beam) and three new cylinders./*Peter Rawson*

Above: One by one the works closed to steam. Doncaster Works' last steam repair job was the now-preserved A4 No 60009, seen there on 6 November 1963./*BR*

Right: Eastleigh's last steam locomotive in for an overhaul was Light Pacific No 34089 *602 Squadron,* highlighted at Waterloo Station on 11 December 1966./*M. Dunnett*

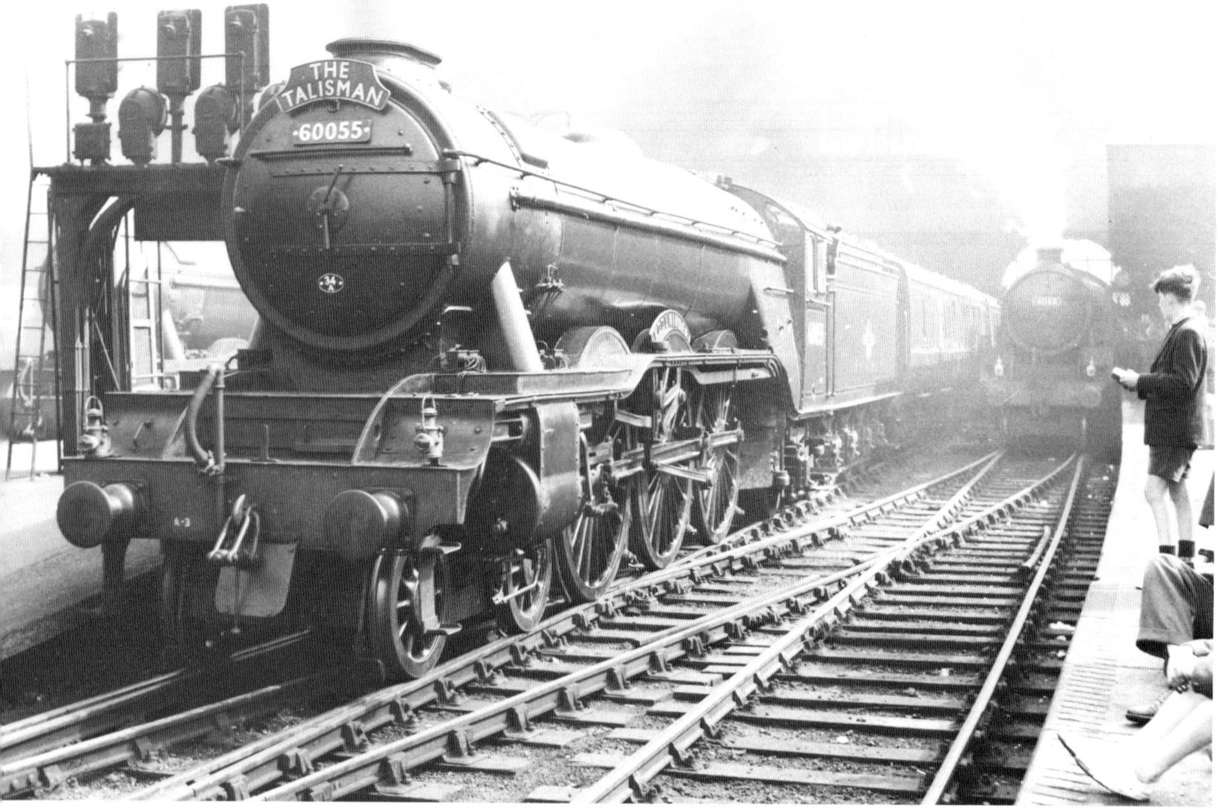
THE TALISMAN
60055

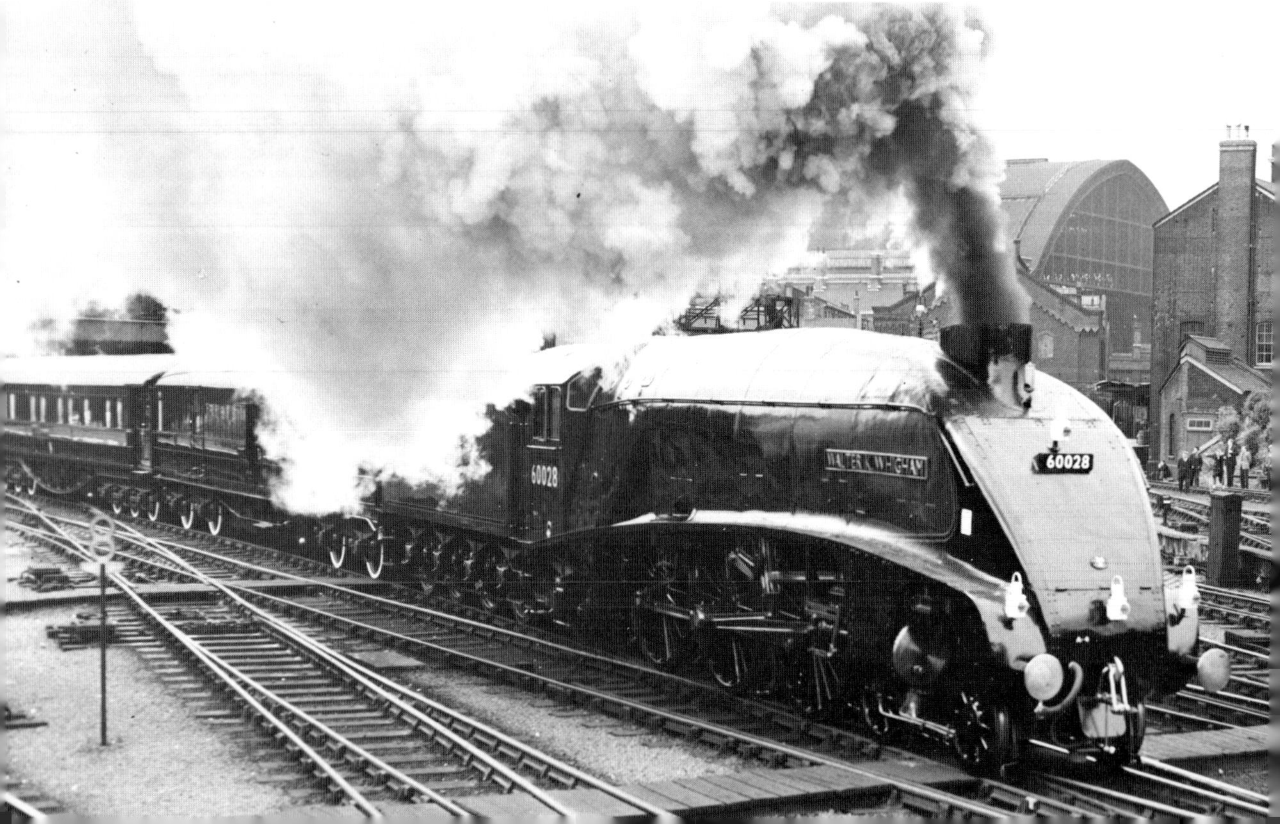
WALTER K. WHIGHAM
60028
60028

East Coast excellence. Kings Cross Top Shed kept its Pacifics hard at it and beautifully turned out. A3 No 60055 *Woolwinder* waiting to leave Kings Cross *(left)* with the down *Talisman* on 3 March 1960. She worked this duty without failure for 21 days. Immaculate A4 No 60028 *(below left)* takes the Royal Train out of the 'Cross' on 8 June 1961 for York./*K. Wheeler; BR*

Steam finale. One of the bright spots of the last years was the A4 haulage of Glasgow-Aberdeen trains. No 60009 near Luncarty *(above)* with the 17.30 ex-Glasgow 3hr express. A memorable day of steam special train working *(below)* on 4 August 1968, at Manchester Victoria. Two LMS 5s, an 8F, a BR 5 and the last 'Britannia'. /*W J.V. Anderson: Bryan H. Jackson*

Steam bows out. *Right:* One of the last steam-hauled passenger trains north of Preston, a Windermere-Carnforth local on 13 July 1968 whose empty stock is being taken through Carnforth. *Below:* An all-too familiar sight in 1967/68 — Carlisle Upperby 'dump' in April 1967./*J. B. Mounsey; Derek Cross*

7
Diesel Engines

It is not intended to describe here how a diesel engine works, because the general principles of an internal combustion engine are very well known in these days of private motorcars and lawn mowers. The diesel engine differs, of course, from the petrol engine mainly in its use of a different fuel and an ignition caused by compressing air to a very high temperature instead of through an electric spark.

During the suction stroke the air required for combustion is drawn into a cylinder through the inlet valve. If, however, it is forced in under pressure, a larger amount is admitted, which allows a greater quantity of fuel to be burned, with consequent greater power. This is called pressure charging, and in the larger engines it is generally done by turbo-blowers driven by exhaust gas. Such blowers can be designed to supply air at pressures of from 4 to 22lb/in^2. Modifications made to naturally-aspirated engines suffice for the lower pressures, with a resulting power increase of from 50 to 60%. This is termed medium pressure charging. For higher charging pressures the engine has to be designed as a pressure-charged unit to withstand the increased stresses. The increase in pressure is of course accompanied by a rise in temperature. When the charging pressure exceeds 15lb/in^2 it is customary to cool the charge air before it enters the cylinders. This results in still greater power by enabling the engine to develop its maximum capability without overheating. The process is called 'charge air cooling' or 'intercooling'. The resulting power increase can be 80% greater than that of a similar but naturally-aspirated engine.[1] High and medium speed engines have already been mentioned, and they represent two trends in the development of the diesel engine. The lightweight high speed engine originated on road vehicles, where high performance in relation to weight was important. The heavier medium speed engine was first used at sea and in stationary plants. The many supporters of the latter claim that it is far the more reliable of the two.

When the number of cylinders does not exceed eight they may be arranged in line, either vertically or horizontally. For higher powers, 12 or 16 cylinders in two vertical banks side by side with separate crankshafts are common. The two banks can also be mounted in V-form with a single crankshaft; the angle between the banks being generally limited to 60° to allow of a walkway on each side. The unusual Deltic form of engine has already been described.

When the Modernisation Plan started the most famous diesel engines outside the USA were those designed by the Swiss firm of Sulzer Brothers. They were therefore an obvious choice for some of the British locomotives, and,

as Sulzers agreed to licence Vickers Armstrong to build any further engines needed after the initial order from Wintherthur, there was no bar to their purchase on the score of their being of foreign manufacture.[2]

Sulzer engines are identified by a code number, which provides fairly full information about the engine; for instance, in the code 12LDA28 the 12 indicates 12 cylinders, the L that it is for locomotive use, the D that it has direct injection, the A that it is turbo-charged, and the 28 that it has a cylinder bore of that diameter in centimetres. To this code a suffix could be added; eg the 12LDA28-A was pressure-charged, while the 12LDA28-B was both pressure-charged and charge air cooled.

The 6-cylinder engine, 6LDA28, is the power unit in the Type 2 diesel-electric locomotives built both by British Railways and the Birmingham Railway Carriage & Wagon Works as part of the order for the original 174 locomotives, and classified respectively at present as 24 and 26. The engine is constructed as a single vertical bank and is pressure-charged, giving 1,160hp at 750 rev/min. The B model of this engine has charge air cooling, and this provides 1,250hp also at 750rev/min. It is the engine of the BR Class 25 and the BRCW Class 27, which are otherwise basically the same as their two respective predecessors. (It is of some interest that a C model of this engine with a horsepower of 1,400 was incorporated in a batch of locomotives built by Tulloch of Sydney for the Commonwealth Railways of Australia in 1964-67.) An 8-cylinder version of this engine, the 8LDA28, powers the Type 3 Class 33 BRCW locomotives of the Southern Region. It is turbo-charged with an output of 1,550hp at 750 rev/min. These large-cylinder and slow-running engines need a lot of headroom and this was obtained by reducing the depth of the underframes.[3] All three of these engines have their cylinders vertically in line with a single crankshaft. Their performance has been excellent and there are no better engines in this power range in the service of British Railways.

Sulzer twin-bank 12-cylinder engines with two crankshafts were fitted to four classes of British Type 4 locomotives: 44, 45, 46, and 47. The first three of these are closely related and are all frequently referred to under the class name of 'Peak' (which strictly speaking belongs only to Class 44). The basic engine is the 12LDA28 which, as originally fitted to the Class 44s, had an output of 2,300hp, making it the most powerful in Western Europe. It was originally a marine design. The 10 engines for the Class 44 were all built by Sulzer at their Winterthur Works in Switzerland. The 183 engines for Classes 45 and 46 were built by Vickers Armstrong at Barrow under sub-contract from Sulzer Brothers. The

Class 44 have the 12LDA28-A which has an exhaust gas pressure charger and provides 2,300hp at 750 rev/min. For the Classes 45 and 46 the engine is uprated to 2,500hp, also at 750 rev/min, by charge air cooling, and is designated 12LDA28-B. These engines are also excellent in performance, but some strains can be set up in the two crankshafts, and this was to be a source of future trouble.[4]

The next uprating of this Sulzer 12-cylinder engine was to 2,750hp, the engine speed being increased to 800 rev/min, for the Class 47 locomotive. The first of this new class was handed over to British Railways towards the end of 1962. Early in 1965 engine troubles occurred in the Western Region; vibrations being set up which the frame members were unable to withstand. This vibration was unexpected because the engines had been used successfully in France and Roumania. However, in neither of those countries had the engines been used to the limit, as they were on British Railways. The reason for the trouble was initially a mystery, and one of the ablest engineers in Great Britain, Sir Arnold Hall (head of the Hawker Siddeley Group to which Brush, the builders of the locomotives belonged) accompanied J.F. Harrison, the CME, on a visit to Sulzer Brothers in Switzerland. The trouble was eventually traced to the fact that Sulzer's had lightened the crankcase webs to bring the engine within the required Class 47 specification. Sulzer's solution was to thicken the webs and replace the engine mounting brackets with a weldless pattern, and also to distribute the stresses. These alterations when put into effect proved satisfactory.[5]

There was an interesting experimental fitting to a batch of Class 47 locomotives of French-built Sulzer 12-cylinder V-type engines of 2,650hp at 1,050 rev/min, designated 12LVA24. The locomotives were re-classified 48. However, in service the V-type engines did not prove as satisfactory as the twin-bank type, and the locomotives were re-engined with the latter, reverting to their 47 classification.

English Electric engines have had a notable record. Ivatt, as mentioned previously, selected English Electric to provide the power for LMS No 10000. It was a 1,600hp V-type pressure-charged engine which had been used successfully on some 1A-Do-A1 locomotives for the Egyptian Railways. It had 16 cylinders and was originally designated 16kV, but this had been changed to 16SIT by the time it was installed in No 10000. The engine speed was 750 rev/min. The firing order of the 10in by 12in cylinders may be of some interest. No 1 cylinder was the furthest from the flywheel to each bank and if the observer faced the engine with the generator on his right and called the bank nearest to him the front (F) and the one furthest away the bank (B), the order was 1F, 8B, 5F, 4B, 7F, 2B, 3F, 6B, 8F, 1B, 4F, 5B, 2F, 7B, 6F, 3B.[6]

The same engine was used for the Southern locomotives Nos 10201 and 10202. For Southern No 10203 the engine was uprated to 2,000hp by increasing the speed to 850 rev/min, and in this form it is the power unit of the English Electric Class 40 locomotives of British Railways and has proved very reliable in service.

The engine of the English Electric Type 1 locomotive (now Class 20) could be considered (like its class number!) to be half the 16SVT, for it is the 8SVT V-type engine of 1,000hp at 850 rev/min. It also has established a reputation of being extremely reliable.

English Electric made its first impact on British Railways with a very large number of Class 08 shunters powered by the 6-cylinder vertical 6KT 350hp engine running at 600 rev/min. Another engine in the lower power range is the 4-cylinder 4SRKT of 500hp at 850 rev/min for the Southern Region diesel-electric multiple-units. Uprated at 600hp, it supplies the diesel power for the Region's very remarkable electro-diesel locomotives of Class 73.

For its Type 3 locomotives, the present Class 37 of British Railways, English Electric provided a 12-cylinder engine, the 12CSVT of 1,750hp at 850rev/min, which is pressure charge and charge air cooled – another excellent design.

For their trial locomotive No DP2 of 1962, English Electric produced a 16-cylinder 16CSVT pressure-charged and charge air cooled engine of 2,700hp at 850rev/min. This was a further development of the engine provided for No 10000. Following the great success of DP2, the same engine was used for the D400 Class (later Class 50) built by English Electric and initially leased to British Railways. However, the airflow had been altered by English Electric and proved unsatisfactory. Conventional oil-wetted air filters were replaced by primary inertia filtration, with secondary filter systems using dry pack elements. These supplied clean air to the engine turbo-blowers, the traction motor blowers, the main generator, and the dynamic brake compartment.[7] R. G. Jarvis, who was then Mechanical Engineer, Design, at Derby, relates that there were many meetings with the English Electric Company concerning the troubles with these engines, which he used to chair. They eventually agreed on a modification to introduce a clean air compartment, more or less on standard lines, and this, as far as Jarvis knows, was reasonably successful.[8]

When it was decided to replace the Mirlees engines of the Brush Type 2 locomotives (Class 31), the English Electric 12-cylinder 12SVT of 1,470hp was selected, a choice which has proved very satisfactory.

English Electric inherited the Deltic engine from the firm of D. Napier & Son, primarily an aero engine company, which they took over in 1942. Lord Nelson, Chairman of English Electric, installed his only son as managing director. The son in due course succeeded his father as the second Lord Nelson and also as head of English Electric. Soon after the war ended, Napier designed and produced both turbo-chargers and the lightweight high-speed Deltic engine. Against considerable opposition from the English Electric Traction Division, Lord Nelson persuaded the Board to make use of the Deltic diesel engine in a locomotive.[9] The two two-stroke engines as fitted in the 'Deltic', or Class 55, locomotive have each 18 cylinders and are designated D18-25. The engine is mechanically blown; that is, there are blowers driven from the engine crankshaft, a system usual with two-stroke engines. Each engine gives 1,650hp at 1,500rev/min. A small Deltic engine, the T9-29 with nine cylinders was provided for a Type 2 locomotive, the Class 23 or so-called 'Baby Deltic'. This engine had an output of 1,100hp at 1,600rev/min.

Considering that the Deltic engine was designed for motor torpedo boats, it performed remarkably well in the Class 55. Harrison says, however, that it cost a lot of money to run. This was not met originally by British Railways because English Electric maintained the engines free for a number of years. By the time that British Railways took over maintenance most of the early troubles had been overcome. Nevertheless Harrison did not think the engine really suitable for railway traction because there were too many component parts.[10] By the time that T. C. B. Miller became CME, British Railways were responsible for looking after them, and Miller described the Deltic engine as excellent in performance but a 'maintenance menace'. He says it cost twice as much to maintain as the normal medium-speed four-stroke engine.

The engine of the 'Baby Deltic' was not even good in performance. In fact it gave so much trouble that the whole class was grounded for a year. The CME, J.F. Harrison, then asked Miller (at that time CM&EE Eastern Region) whether it was worth trying these locomotives again. As Napier had been putting in a lot of hard work on them, Miller replied that he thought it was. They then did a fair amount of useful work, but were eventually scrapped as being unreliable. The 'Baby Deltics' had the same size cylinders as the Deltics, but the engine ran at 1,600rev/min, as compared with the 1,500rev/min of the Deltic, and the cylinder hp was 122, whilst the Deltic only produced 92. The trouble may have been partly due to this difference.[11] In the opinion of R. C. Bond, the Deltics were worth their cost in maintenance because of their fine performance, and he thinks the 'Baby Deltic' engines may have been under developed.[12]

There was an odd 'might-have-been' in connection with the 'Baby Deltic' locomotive. In 1958 English Electric started design work on a high-speed 12-cylinder engine which it was intended should, in its final stage of development, produce 2,700hp at from 1,500 to 1,800rev/min. This became known as the U engine. It was intended primarily for the overseas market, for English Electric were well aware that high-speed engines were regarded with little favour by British Railways. In May 1963 the first model of the engine was ready for trials, producing at this stage 1,550hp at 1,500rev/min. After completing its trials successfully, its installation in a suitable locomotive was discussed with British Railways, with the result that one of the 'Baby Deltics' was selected – the withdrawal of the whole class having started. In October 1963 the locomotive was ready to receive its U engine, but at that stage changes in the management of both the Diesel Engine and Traction Divisions of English Electric resulted in a change of attitude to the project, and in December 1965 all further work on it ceased.[13]

In 1968 the following companies merged: General Electric (GEC), English Electric, and Associated Electrical Industries (AEI); the last of these being the combination of British Thomson-Houston (BTH) and Metropolitan Vickers (Metrovick). The organisation that eventually resulted from that merger into an enlarged GEC was roughly as follows. Under GEC a number of subsidiary companies were formed, of which the most important in relation to railway traction were GEC Traction Ltd and GEC Diesels Ltd. The latter of these consisted of three semi-independent components. Ruston Diesels Ltd dealing with the English Electric medium speed engines, Paxman Diesels Ltd making Paxman and Deltic high speed engines, and Dorman Diesels Ltd for the very high speed low power engines of that name.

The new English Electric engine range is known as the RK series, and it consists of two types: the RK3XT which is turbo-charged and the RK3CT which is turbo-charged and charge air cooled. Of the latter type the 16-cylinder 16RK3CT with a rating of 3,520hp at 900rev/min has been chosen by British Railways for the new Class 56 heavy freight locomotive; though it is set at 3,250hp. The engine is a still further development of that fitted in No 10000.

Paxman engines have had something of a mixed history in British Railways service. The BTH Type 1 locomotive, later Class 15, and NBL Type 1, of a class which did not last long enough to get a numerical classification, both had the Paxman 16-cylinder 16YHXL V-type pressure-charge engine of 800hp at 1,250rev/min, and neither class can be rated as a success. One of the British Railways Type 4 locomotives of the 'Warship' class, No 830, was given two Paxman 12-cylinder engines of type 12YKXL, each of 1,200 hp at 1,500rev/min, but the experiment was not repeated. Clayton's Type 1 locomotive of 1962, which became Class 17, had two 6-cylinder Paxman 6ZHXL, each of 450hp at 1,500rev/min. These were pressure-charged horizontal engines which Miller says had been developed for railcars and there was every reason to suppose that they would be good; but they were not.[14] Harrison says that this flat engine was a bad design. There were camshaft failures, the engine needed balancing, there was fretting corrosion between generator flange and engine, too much aluminium had been used in construction, and the turbo-charger bearings failed often and kept availability down to something like 50% – 'an appalling figure'.[15]

Miller, as CME, had the responsibility of deciding on the engine of the High Speed Train. The Chief Engineer had ruled that trains running at the speed envisaged must not have an axle load greater than 16.5 tons. This entailed having engines of light weight, and these, to provide the power required, would in Miller's opinion have to be high speed. He did not want a foreign engine and the only maker of high-speed engines of the requisite power was the GEC subsidiary, Paxman.[16] Jarvis confirms that there was indeed little choice. The power cars would have to be either Bo-Bos of about 70 tons with a high speed engine, or, if a medium-speed engine was used, Co-Cos weighing about 115 tons (an extra 90 tons for two power cars, which was worth three carriages).[17]

The Paxman Ventura engine provided a basis of development, and, as the Admiralty was also interested, both they and British Railways worked on the design in conjunction with Paxman.[18] The result was the Paxman Valenta with an improved crankshaft. It is a 12-cylinder

V-type engine, pressure-charged and intercooled, designated 12RP200L, and develops 2,250hp at 1,500rev/min. For its weight the Valenta is the most highly-rated diesel engine in traction service, and the output of this 8-ton engine is only equalled by that of a 30 ton medium speed diesel engine.[19] Miller says that it performed very well during the long period of trial with the prototype HST but that some design weaknesses became apparent in service.[20] These weaknesses lay mainly, apparently, in the connecting rods and turbo-chargers, and the engines had to be temporarily derated.[21] The normal rating has now however been restored.[22]

Paxman Diesels Ltd have given details of a single-bank 6-cylinder variant of the Valenta, rated at 1,255hp at 1,500rev/min, which has been developed jointly with British Railways for above-floor fitting in the prototype diesel-electric multiple-units of Class 210.[23]

Brush equipped their A1A-A1A Type 2 locomotives (now Class 31) with the Mirlees diesel engine. In 1948 there had been a merger of oil engine manufacturers, embracing Brush, Petters Ltd (which was already Brush controlled) with Mirlees, Bickerton & Day, J. H. McLaren Ltd, and Oil Engine (Coventry) Ltd. The combine was called the Brush Associated British Oil Engine Group, and it had a common chairman. Thus, with a single control over engines, electrical equipment, and mechanical parts, the Brush Company could build complete locomotives and could seek orders.

Ivatt had retired from the LMS when Nationalisation came and joined the Brush Electrical Engineering Company as a consultant. It was after his arrival that the company began to build main line diesel locomotives. R.C. Bond says that Ivatt brought to Brush a great deal of experience and had considerable influence on what the firm did.[24] The first Brush main line diesel locomotives were 25 A1A-A1A type for the Ceylon Government Railways, with 12-cylinder V-type Mirlees engines of 1,000hp at 850rev/min. In 1955, in the light of the Ceylon success and the knowledge that Ivatt had a hand on the helm, British Railways included an order for 20 Brush Type 2 locomotives in the first 174. They had the same Mirlees engine (JVS12T) as had been fitted to the Ceylon locomotives, but at its normal condition rating of 1,250hp instead of the 1,000hp rating required by Ceylon. It had been designed originally as a marine engine and had been so used before its introduction to railway service.

In July 1958 another 40 Brush Type 2s were ordered, but in these the engines were uprated to 1,365hp by increasing the speed to 900rev/min. One of the new batch had its engine uprated still further to 1,600hp by increasing the speed again to 950rev/min, and 20 more locomotives were ordered with this higher rating. With this power they were Type 3, rather than Type 2. Out of 66 further locomotives ordered, five were of 1,600hp and the remainder 1,365hp. The last order was placed in 1961, and in one of these locomotives the Mirlees engine was temporarily uprated to 2,000hp by intercooling, thus bringing it into the Type 4 category.

However, the Mirlees engines, which had hitherto given good service, were now suffering from fatigue troubles.

Miller says that even the 1,250hp engines began to break up, and adds that it was due largely to fractures in the crankcase. A great deal of research was undertaken to see what could be done, though Miller believes that it was not carried far enough. He thinks that if the researches had been pursued the Mirlees engines could have been made satisfactory.[25] In 1964 British Railways began replacing the Mirlees engine by one of English Electric design, as already related. The Mirlees company took back the engines and subsequently sold them for installation in trawlers — back into the marine service for which they had been originally designed and in which they were very successful.[26]

Similar troubles with the Mirlees engine occurred in a batch of 14 1,750hp Co-Co locomotives ordered in 1961 by Rhodesia Railways, but in this case the crankcases were replaced by steel ones supplied by Mirlees and fitted by Rhodesia Railways.[27]

The story of the Crossley engine is rather sad. In 1955 Metropolitan-Vickers received an order from the Western Australian Government Railways for 48 mixed traffic locomotives of the 2-Do-2 wheel arrangement for their 3ft 6in gauge system. The diesel engine selected was a two-stroke 8-cylinder V-type, model HST V-8, designed and built by Crossley Brothers Ltd of Manchester, with a system known as Exhaust Pulse Pressure Charging, by which much of the inlet air which passes through into the exhaust during scavenging, is forced back into the cylinder by the impulse pressure of the exhaust gases from another cylinder; thus increasing the quantity and pressure of the inlet air trapped by the rising piston. A valuable feature was that this result was achieved without any mechanism. The maximum service speed of the locomotive was 55mile/h. All 48 were delivered in 1954 and in 1978 the whole lot were still in service — the biggest class by far on the WAGR 3ft 6in gauge, and at 24 years of age this is already well beyond what is normally expected of a diesel locomotive. Their success in traffic was immediate, and they cut the fastest steam timing of 16.5 hours between Perth and Kalgoorlie by four hours.

In 1954, a year later than the above order, Metrovick received one from CIE, the Irish Transport Company, for 94 locomotives with Crossley engines, of which 60 were to be of 1,200hp and 34 of 550hp. The former had the same engine as those of the WAGR, and with the same speed, but uprated. This 1,200hp engine was also installed in the Co-Bo Metrovick locomotives of Class 28 ordered by British Railways, of which the first was delivered in 1958. On neither British nor Irish Railways were the engines a success. Bond says that they were quite unreliable,[28] and on the Irish locomotives they were replaced by General Motors engines. It may be that the uprating of the engine was a mistake.

Travelling from Waterford to Rosslare, I found one of the larger Metrovick locomotives, still with its Crossley engine, at the head of the train in Waterford station; and in discussion with the driver I was misguided enough to query the ability of his locomotive to run fast. Those who know this line, with its succession of reverse curves which made eating in the Great Southern & Western restaurant cars of the boat trains a precarious business, will appreciate how misguided was this suggestion to an Irish driver. My poor wife suffered more than I did, and we moved from an end compartment to one in the middle of the train in the hope that our baggage might remain on the racks. At Rosslare I passed a beaming driver, who obviously expected a congratulatory word, and I had not the heart to disappoint him!

Most of the locomotives constructed by the North British Locomotive Company had the MAN engine which they built under licence. Bond thinks that NBL would have done better to have bought the engines from MAN, rather than building themselves,[29] if the difficulty over foreign manufacture could have been overcome. The MAN 12-cylinder L12V18/21 engine was installed in four types of locomotives: the NBL Type 4 A1A-A1A 'Warship' class, British Railways B-B 'Warship' class, and two NBL Type 2 classes, of which one had hydraulic transmission and the other electric. The engines varied slightly, being of either 1,000 or 1,100hp at 1,445 or 1,500rev/min, the Type 4s having two of them. Bond says that all these engines gave trouble, although those in the Type 4s were rather less troublesome than the ones in the Type 2s.

The other German high-speed engine was the Maybach, manufactured under licence by Bristol Siddeley. Most of the British Railways Class 42 'Warships' had Maybachs, as did also the Class 52 'Westerns' and Class 35 'Hymeks'. The 'Warships' had two 12-cylinder MD650V model engines of 1,056hp at 1,400 rev/min (of which some were later uprated to 1,152hp at 1,530rev/min). The 'Westerns' had two 12-cylinder MD655 engines of 1,350hp at 1,500rev/min, and the 'Hymeks' had a single 16-cylinder MD870 engine of 1,700hp at 1,500rev/min. These Maybach engines were much better than the NBL-manufactured MAN engines and performed satisfactorily in service.

Notes

1 Doherty, J. M.; *Diesel Locomotive Practice;* London, Odhams Press, 1963, pp25, 119-120.
2 Harrison, J. F.; Information to the Author
3 Doherty, op cit, p41
4 ibid
5 ibid
6 British Railways brochures, 1949
7 GEC Traction Limited, *2700hp Diesel-Electrics for British Rail* (reprint from *Railway Gazette* 5 April 1968)
8 Jarvis, R. G.; Information to the Author
9 Webb, Brian; *The English Electric Main Line Diesels of British Rail;* Newton Abbot, David & Charles, 1976, p28
10 Harrison, J. F.; Information to the Author
11 Miller, T. C. B. Information to the Author
12 Bond, R. C.; Information to the Author
13 Tufnell, R. M.; The Engine that never Ran a Mile, *General Engineer,* vol89, p249
14 Miller, T. C. B, Information to the Author
15 Harrison, J. F., Information to the Author
16 Miller T. C. B., op cit
17 Jarvis, R. G. op cit
18 Miller, T. C. B.; op cit
19 *Railway World,* February 1979, p105
20 Miller T. C. B.; op cit
21 Bond, R. C.; op cit
22 *Railway World,* op cit
23 ibid
24 Bond, R. C.; op cit
25 Miller, T. C. B.; op cit
26 ibid
27 Toms, George; *Brush Diesel Locomotives 1940-78;* Sheffield, Turntable Publications, 1978, p96
28 Bond, R. C.; op cit
29 ibid

Below: Very new, BRCW Type 2 No D5300 pulls away from Welwyn Garden City with empty stock in September 1958./*C.R.L. Coles*

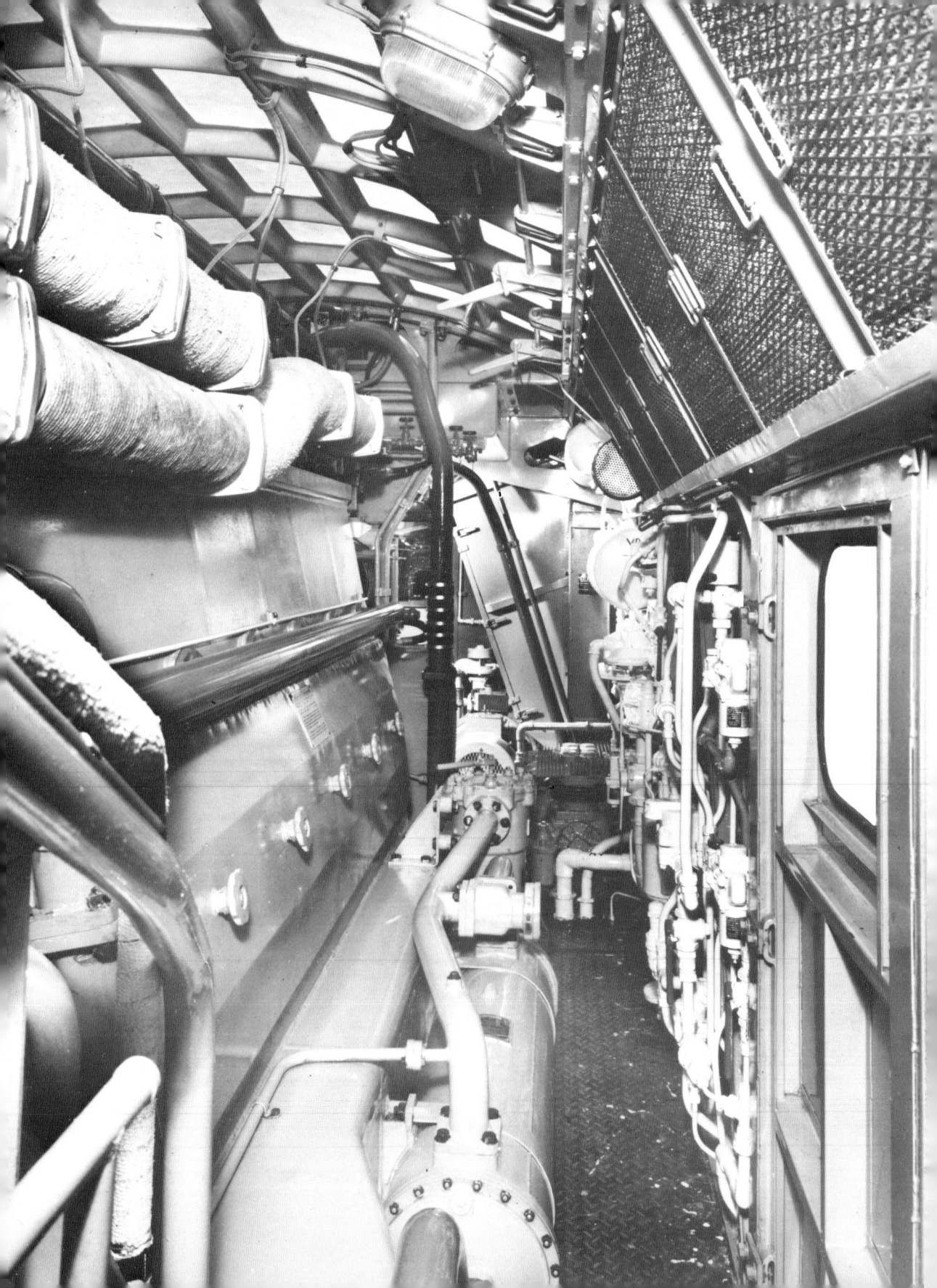

Left: A diesel engine in place in a locomotive. A Sulzer 6-cylinder 6LDA28 in a Birmingham BRCW-built Type 2.
/Railway Industry Association

Two views of diesel engine manufacturers' production. *Right:* North British Locomotive Co's Diesel Engine Division MAN engine erecting shop. *Below:* Mirlees JVS12T engine with generators attached undergoing test runs at the Mirlees plant./*Railway Industry Association/Hawker Siddeley*

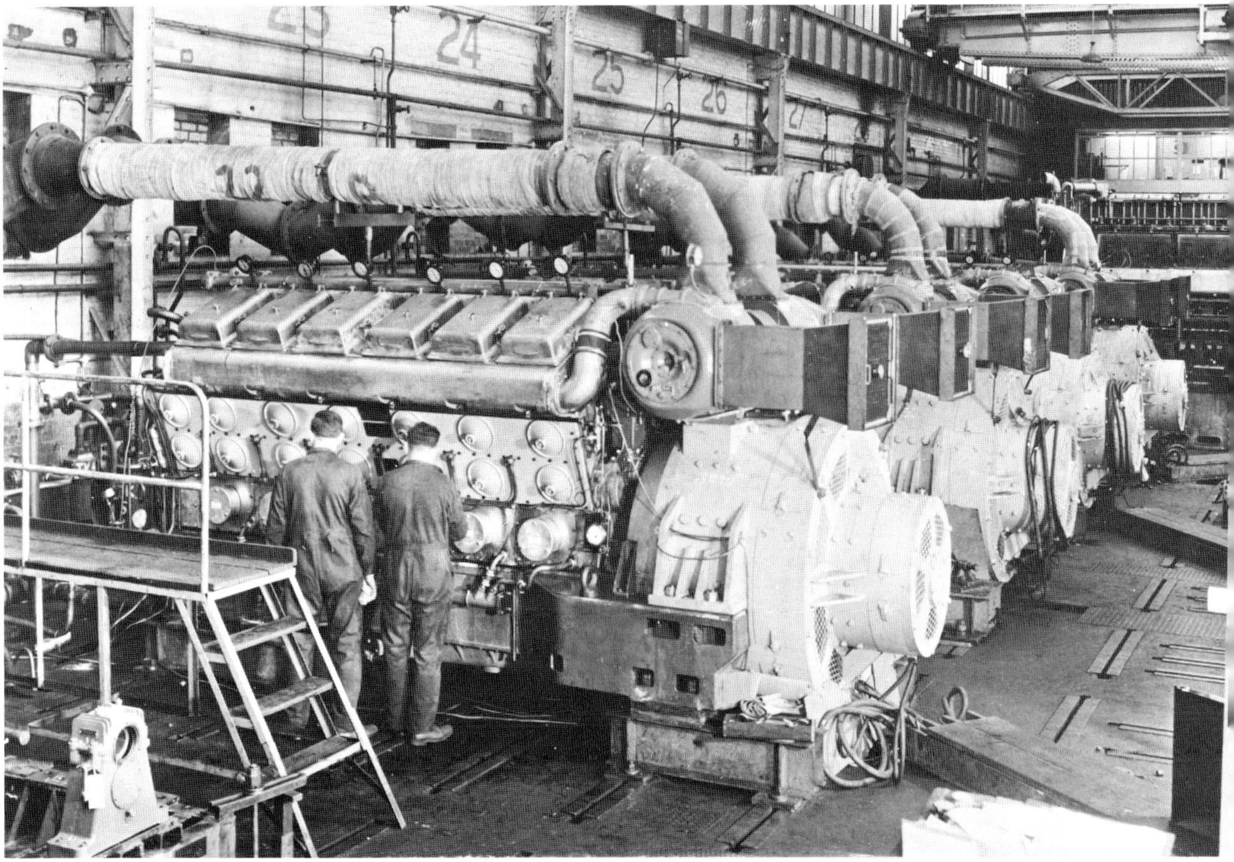

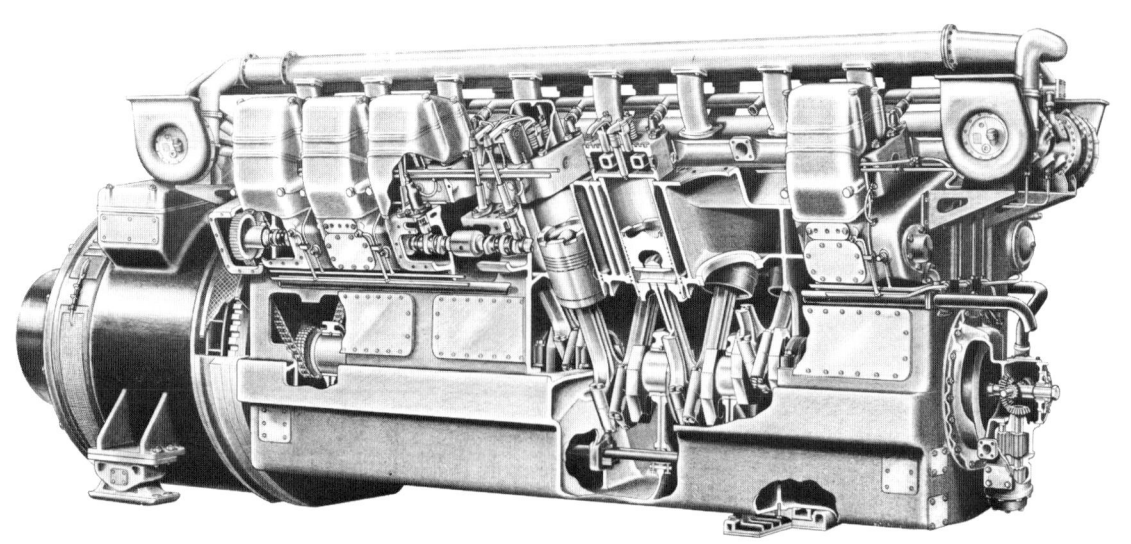

Two more diesel power units. *Left:* The English Electric 16SVT. *Below left:* The Sulzer 6LDA28./*Both: GEC*

Right: A big moment at Barrow when Dr Beeching, then BR's Chairman, accepts delivery of the 1,000th Sulzer diesel engine manufactured under licence by Vickers. /*Railway Industry Association*

Below: Class 47 No 1506 at speed on an up East Coast express, near Beningborough in 1974./*John E. Oxley*

Bottom: Nothing to tell from the outside but D1703 had one of the French-built 2,650hp V-type Sulzer engines when photographed in 1969./*D.L. Percival*

Above: The 16CSVT engine in the English Electric prototype Type 4. No DP2, powers it along the West Coast main line in the early 1960s. */GEC*

Below: An early view of one of the production 'Deltics' in East Coast service, on an up express near Hatfield./*GEC*

Above right: The new BR Class 56 has the 16RK3CT engine built by Ruston Diesels, part of GEC. No 56.049 passes through Leamington on a Didcot-bound coal train in May 1979./*Paul Harris*

Centre right: A rare view of the Paxman engined diesel-electric railcar set of the late 1950s, here approaching Hellifield during trials over the Settle & Carlisle line in January 1958./*Ian Allan Library*

Bottom right: Mirlees-engined Brush Type 2 No D5516 in 1959. */Sam Lambert*

The unhappy Metrovick Co-Bos. *Left:* D5700 ex-works. *Below:* On acceptance tests, having been built at Stockton, No D5702 heads a test train through East Boldon bound for Sunderland in September 1958./*GEC; I.S. Carr*

Right: MAN-engined No D600./*Sam Lambert*

Below right: A look at an ill-starred diesel prototype – Sulzer-engined BRCW/AEI 2,750hp prototype *Lion*, hauling a down WR main line parcels train near Twyford in July 1962./*Cecil J. Blay*

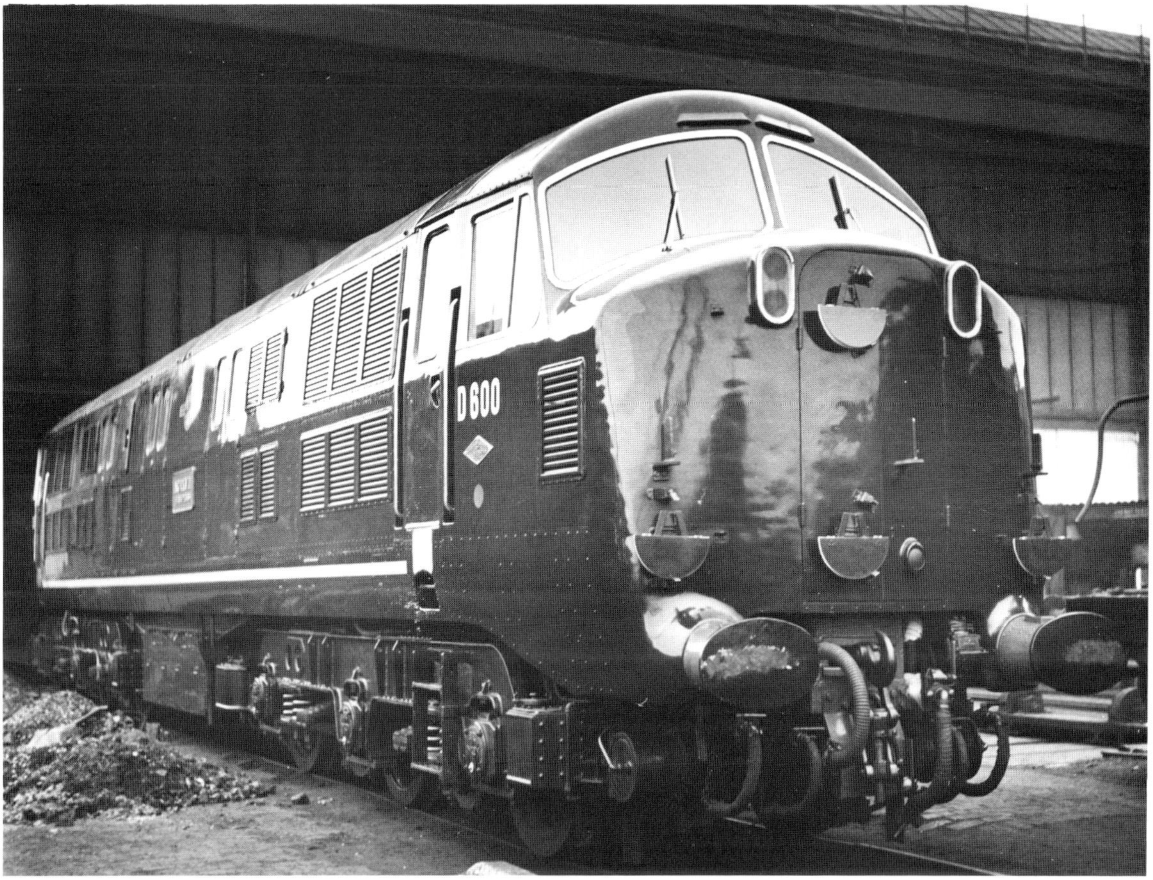
D600

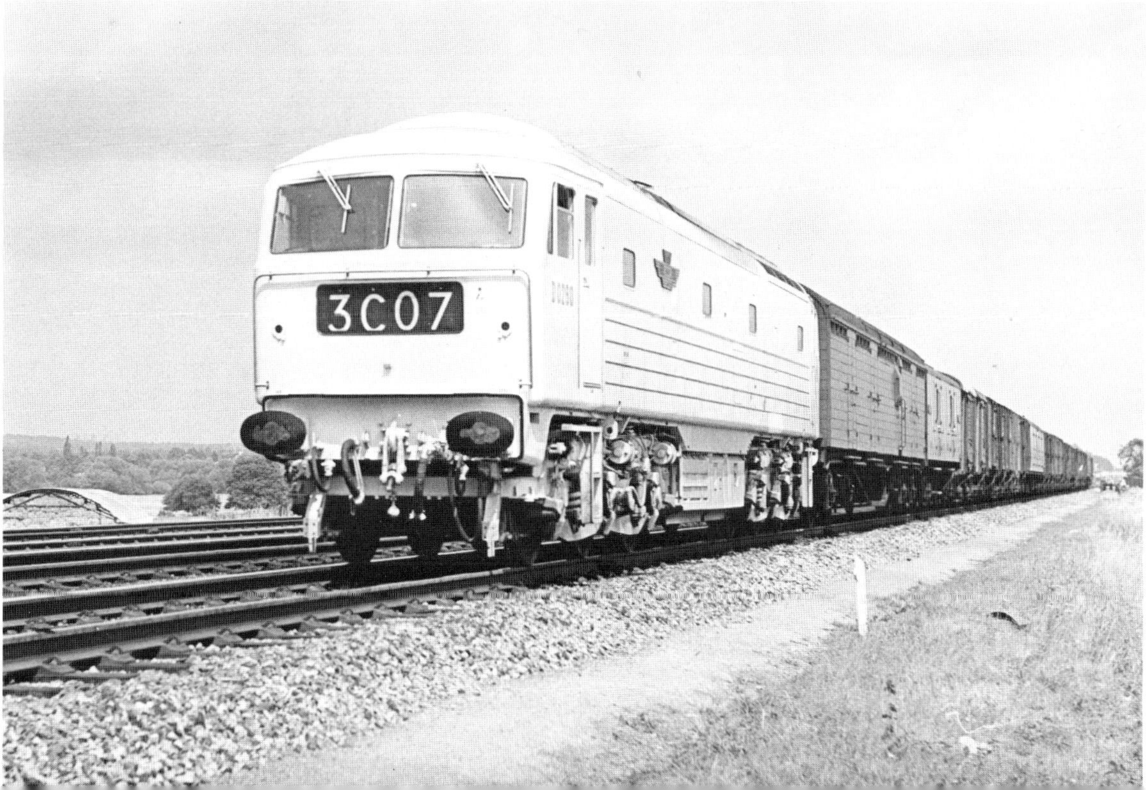
3C07

8
Diesel Locomotives

The last Chapter dealt with the diesel engine, which can perhaps be considered as the equivalent of the boiler of a steam locomotive, in that it provides the 'steam' which makes the locomotive work. Here we are concerned with the locomotive as a whole.

It is probably most convenient to consider the various locomotive classes in the ascending order of the power types under which they were originally ordered, that is: Type 1, 1,000hp or less; Type 2, above 1,000hp and under 1,500hp; Type 3, 1,500hp and under 2,000hp; Type 4, 2,000hp and under 3,000hp; and Type 5, 3,000hp and above.

Type 1

The first of the Type 1 locomotives to be received by British Railways was No D8000, an English Electric Bo-Bo locomotive of a series now known as Class 20. The original order was for 20, all of which were built at English Electric's Vulcan Foundry at Newton-le-Willows, north of Warrington. The main generator of the locomotive feeds the four axle-hung nose-suspended traction motors, while the auxiliary generator provides supplies for battery charging, the air compressor for the locomotive air brake, the sanding gear, the air horns, the electro-pneumatic control gear, the train vacuum brake exhauster, and the traction motor ventilation blowers. The superstructure is of the hood or bonnet type, with a full width driving cab at one end. The locomotives normally work with the cab leading because of the restricted visibility if the bonnet leads. The D8000s were intended primarily for freight working, so they have no train heating boiler, but with a maximum speed of 75 mile/h they are quite capable of working passenger trains in the summer months, and have frequently been so used. The 20 locomotives were delivered in 1957-58 and all went to the London Midland Region and were allocated to the Devons Road depot at Bow, which was the first depot on British Railways to be turned over completely to diesel motive power. After being tried out for a time on London area freight trains, a number were dispersed throughout Great Britain for experience and driver training. Bond says that they are excellent locomotives and have never given any trouble.[1] It was not long therefore before further orders followed, until 128 were delivered, the last in July 1962. No more were ordered for a time because of the one major disadvantage, the poor visibility when running with bonnet leading. This of course happened frequently when shunting, even though it was generally possible to arrange for the cab end to lead when hauling trains. British Railways had found an attractive alternative in the Clayton Equipment Company's 900hp Bo-

Bo locomotive with a centre cab and a low bonnet fore and aft. Following the failure of this design, because of its poor engines, orders for another 100 of Class 20 were placed, and these were delivered from 1966 to 1968. The Class 20 locomotives have achieved the remarkable figure of 90% availability, which is greater than any other diesel class on British Railways.[2]

There were two other Type 1 classes in the early orders, neither of which were particularly distinguished and they merit only brief mention. They were both Bo-Bo diesel electrics and both had the Paxman 800hp engine described in the previous chapter. The main contractor of one class (D8200, later Class 15) was British Thomson Houston, who supplied the electrical equipment. The mechanical strucure was designed, and the bogies and superstructure were built, by the Clayton Equipment Company. The North British Locomotive Company was the main contractor for the other class, D8400, the electrical equipment for which was supplied by GEC. Both classes had long bonnets, but they also had short ones on the other side of the cab. Only 10 were originally ordered for each class, but, owing to the acceleration of the diesel programme, following the abolition of the three-year trial period, another 34 of the D8200's were ordered. No more of the D8400's were built and all were scrapped before the numerical classification system was introduced. Bond rates both classes as adequate but not outstanding.[3]

The last Type 1 to be built was Clayton's central cab locomotive mentioned above. It was a Bo-Bo diesel electric with GEC electrical equipment (except for some equipped by Crompton Parkinson) and with a central cab which gave excellent visibility over the two low bonnets. Each bonnet housed one of the two engines, and in shunting it could, if desired, work on only one of them. It looked so good and first tests were so promising that its ultimate failure was something of a tragedy. A total of 117 were built, starting in 1962, but the engines were so poor that some of the class were scrapped within three years of their first appearance,[4] though others lasted long enough to acquire the numerical classification of 17.

Type 2

The first of the Type 2 classes to enter service on British Railways was the excellent Brush diesel-electric design with six axles in the A1A-A1A wheel arrangement, originally classed D5500 and later 31. The first locomotive of the class was handed over to British Railways in October 1957. The electrical equipment is by Brush, and there are four nose-suspended axle-hung and force ventilated traction motors. The original order had been for 20 locomotives, but they performed such useful service that building went on until there were eventually 263, the last being delivered in 1962. T. C. B. Miller says that they were the backbone of Great Eastern line motive power when it was converted to diesel operation. East Anglia was, in fact, the first area in Great Britain to be completely dieselised, when, says Miller, 246 diesel locomotives replaced 660 steam locomotives of all sorts, types, and classes and with a fuel bill reduced by half for the same amount of work.[5]

British Railways' order for these locomotives was due to a great extent, as had been said, to Ivatt's part in Brush diesel-electric design. The unmotored carrying wheels were necessary because of the locomotive's comparatively high weight of 104 tons. The 31s have a high maximum speed of 90 mile/h and are as much at home on light express trains as fairly heavy goods trains. As already recorded, trouble that eventually developed in the Mirlees engines led them all to be replaced by English Electric engines, and this alteration was applied to the whole fleet during the period 1965-1969.

Many of these fine locomotives have now been transferred to the Western Region, where they may be seen on all sorts of duties from hauling fast passenger trains to working empty carriage stock into Paddington station.

The British Railways design of Type 2 mixed traffic locomotives has turned out to be one of the most numerous and useful classes. The first of an order for 20, No D5000, arrived at Marylebone on 14 July 1958 for official inspection. Further orders followed, and these excellent diesel-electric locomotives, which became Class 24, eventually numbered 150. The electrical equipment is by BTH. The following year the engine was uprated from 1,160 to 1,250hp, and 325 more were built. This more powerful version is now Class 25.

The first 30 of Class 24 were built at Derby, but subsequent batches of both classes were built at Crewe and Darlington, as well as at Derby. They were intended for mixed traffic work on the London Midland Region, and they can be regarded as the modern replacement for the LMS and BR Class 5 4-6-0s. (It is a happy coincidence that their original numbers should have been in the 5000 series.) The first 20 were employed from the start on the Midland line services between Derby and Manchester, with extensions to and from Liverpool over the old Cheshire Lines. Some of the later batches went temporarily to the Eastern and North Eastern Regions; and Southern Region had some until their own Class 33s were ready. Of the 25s, 54 were ordered from Beyer Peacock in 1964, but this grand old firm had to close the locomotive side of their business, and they only built 37. Nevertheless, in the opinion of some, the Beyer Peacock locomotives were the best of the lot.[6] The majority of these locomotives do not have steam heating, and none are being fitted for electric train heating. The maximum speed of the 24s was 75 mile/h, but the 25s can run at 90 mile/h. The later Class 25s were fitted with a different traction motor which, following the merger of BTH and Metrovick design, was designated AEI. It is smaller and more compact, but certain troubles were experienced with it on the Western Region through overheating when two

locomotives were used in multiple on 990 ton iron ore trains. The troubles disappeared when the train loads were reduced to 810 tons.[7]

Nearly all the Class 24s have been withdrawn at the time of writing, but over 300 of the 25s are still running. Most of them are still on the London Midland Region, though Western Region acquired some when their Class 22 diesel-hydraulics were withdrawn, and allocated them to Plymouth (Laira), Bristol and Newport.[8]

Very similar to the above two classes are the Bo-Bo diesel-electric locomotives built by the Birmingham Railway Carriage & Wagon Company. Class 26 have the same engine as Class 24, and Class 27 the same as that of Class 26. Of Class 26, 20 locomotives formed part of the original order for 174, but more were ordered after the abandonment of the three-year trial period. Trials would have been carried out to see whether the BR or the BRCW design was the better, but owing to the acceleration of the dieselisation programme, both types had to be ordered. Fortunately they were both good, and there were ultimately 47 of Class 26 and 69 of Class 27. Bond says that they were every bit as good as the pair designed by British Railways.[9] Maximum speeds are 80 mile/h for Class 26 and 90 mile/h for Class 27.

By 1970 both classes had been concentrated in Scotland and for some time they almost monopolised the Highland and West Highland main lines. It was one day when he was about to return from Wick behind one of them that Bond was struck with the great advantage that diesel locomotives have over steam in being immediately available without having to undergo the lengthy process of raising steam.[10]

I have encountered these locomotives at Crianlarich, Oban, Fort William, Mallaig, Inverness, and Kyle of Lochalsh, and indeed at this period I never saw any other type in the Highlands. From their numbers I knew them as the '53s' and, to my astonishment, I acquired quite an affection for them — influenced perhaps by the lovely scenery through which they ran. Watching two of them taking a train out of Crianlarich station over the viaduct on the West Highland line, they recalled in an odd way two of the North British 'Glen' class 4-4-0s, which so often double-headed a train over this same viaduct.

In 1970 24 locomotives of Class 27 were modified to work a high-speed push-pull express service between Edinburgh and Glasgow with one locomotive at each end of the train. Services began in May 1971, but a number of troubles were encountered before these essentially mixed traffic locomotives settled down to operating the genesis of the High Speed Train.

All the remaining Type 2 classes were failures on account of the troubles with their engines, which have been dealt with in the previous chapter. These were the English Electric Class 23 'Baby Deltics', the North British Locomotive Company's Bo-Bo diesel-electrics of Class 21 and B-B diesel-hydraulics of Class 22 with Voith transmission, and the Metrovick Co-Bos of Class 28. All of them have been scrapped. The Metrovick locomotive was a particular disappointment because Bond was interested both in its two-stroke engine and in the five axles of the two bogies to cater for an engine weight which was just too much for four axles yet not enough for six. They were nice looking locomotives and Metrovick had done well as builders of electrical locomotives and equipment. Re-engined they would probably have been as good as their Irish sisters. However, British Railways had more than enough different types without adding to them!

Type 3

The Type 3 locomotives built by the Birmingham Railway Carriage & Wagon Works for the Southern Region, later Class 33, have been very successful and are still the Southern's only standard diesel locomotive. To the casual eye the 33 looks exactly the same as the 26 and 27, and indeed the body has the same dimensions and weight, and the Crompton Parkinson electrical equipment is the same. The reason for this similarity, in spite of the increased power, is that no boiler for steam heating was required so that there was room to install an 8-cylinder instead of a 6-cylinder Sulzer engine. The locomotives were intended primarily for freight and for use on the heavier summer passenger traffic when heating is not required. However, provision was made for electric train heating and this caters for all modern hauled carriage stock. A total of 98 Class 33 locomotives were built between 1960 and 1962.

Perhaps the most interesting use of the 33s is in connection with the Bournemouth line electrification. A Bournemouth and Weymouth express leaves Waterloo with 12 coaches, made up of two 4-coach trailer sets (Class 491) leading, followed by a 4-coach motor set (Class 430) with eight 348hp motors (a total of 2,784 hp) which propels the train from the rear. On arrival at Bournemouth, which is the end of the electrified section, the Class 430 set is uncoupled and either one or both 491 sets are hauled on to Weymouth by a 33. On the up service the procedure is reversed; the 33 propelling the 491s to Bournemouth, where they are attached to the 430, which then pulls them to Waterloo. It is a measure of the status of the 33s (which might almost be described as replacements for the 'King Arthurs') that the Southern Region is to give them names; though at the time of writing these had not been announced.

From 1967 the unreliability of the Western Region's Type 4 diesel-hydraulic 'Warships' of Class 42, led to the 33s supplementing them on the Waterloo-Exeter services. In 1971 the 33s took over completely the working of these services and have been used on them exclusively ever since. Southern enthusiasts doubtless consider them a far more appropriate motive power for the old London & South Western Railway's main line to the West. One can well imagine the indignation of Dugald Drummond at seeing the products of Swindon working trains over the racing track of his beautiful engines.

In the opinion of T. C. B. Miller, the Class 37 Co-Co diesel-electrics built by English Electric are the most reliable and best all-round diesel locomotives on British Railways,[11] and R. C. Bond rates them as first class and just better than Class 33.[12] No less than 308 were built between 1960 and 1963, and they can be seen working passenger and freight trains all over British Railways. Perhaps their nearest steam equivalents were Gresley's V2 class 2-6-2s on the LNER. They have the appearance

which Bond insisted on when he was CME, for the larger locomotives, with a 'nose' at each end and which is common to the Class 40s, the 'Peaks', and the 'Deltics'. They have a maximum speed of 90 mile/h and have been used, like the V2s, on some of the fastest passenger trains. In 1965 the Western Region carried out high speed trials with two 37s in multiple between Paddington, Bristol, and Plymouth. On one of the test runs in the up direction there was a special easing of the 90 mile/h limit and maximum speeds of 102 mph and 104 mile/h respectively were recorded on two occasions between Challow and Goring.[13]

The traction motors are the same as those fitted on the 'Deltics' and are interchangeable with them; the bogies too are generally similar to those of the 'Deltics'.[14]

The remaining Type 3 were the Class 35, or 'Hymek', B-B diesel locomotives with hydro-mechanical (Mekydro) transmission, built by Beyer Peacock in 1961, and intended primarily to replace steam locomotives in the Bristol area, South Wales, and west of Newton Abbot on all services; undertaking the kind of duties at one time performed mostly by Great Western 'Halls' and Moguls. A total of 101 were built, but although they worked very successfully all over the Western Region, Bond says that they were inferior to the Class 37s.[15] Harrison adds that there were a number of Mekydro transmission failures when operating freight trains, caused by reverse torques. Like all Beyer Peacock products, they were very well built. It was the cessation of orders for the 'Hymeks' which caused Beyer Peacock to close down the locomotive part of their business. All the 'Hymeks' have now been withdrawn.

Type 4

In March 1958 British Railways received the first of the Type 4 locomotives ordered under the modernisation plan. It was No D200, a 1Co-Co1 diesel-electric built by English Electric, the progenitor of a series of 200 locomotives which were to become Class 40. D200 was a direct development of No 10000, but, to carry its greater weight, the bogie designed for the Southern Railway main line diesel-electrics was used.

The first batch went to the Eastern Region for use on the Great Eastern section. On 18 March 1958 No D200 hauled a nine-coach passenger train on a demonstration run from Liverpool Street to Norwich and back. A board on the front of the train was emblazoned with British Railways' demi-lion rampant and wheel badge and the legend 'FIRST 2000hp DIESEL LONDON-NORWICH: progress by GREAT EASTERN'; a charming piece of nostalgic propaganda which delighted lovers of the old Great Eastern Railway and its 'Claud Hamiltons'. Before the end of the year and the new locomotives were working not only on the most important East Anglian expresses but were appearing on the principal East Coast services. Then on the London Midland Region the D200s took over many of the main line services from Euston, and by 1961 they were working about 80% of the West Coast expresses; though the 'Royal Scot' was usually hauled by LMS Pacifics until their withdrawal in 1964![16] Their employment on trains between Euston and Liverpool led to 25 of them being named after liners of the great shipping companies trading to and from Liverpool; a revival of an idea which resulted in 'Teutonic' class compounds of the London & North Western Railway being named after White Star liners.

Compared to more modern diesel power the D200s, or Class 40, are very heavy (133 tons) for their 2,000hp, but they are among the most reliable of British Railways' diesel locomotives, and they were invaluable during the early period of enforced rapid transition from steam. In addition, their powers of acceleration shortened the recovery time needed, when the electrification work from Euston to Liverpool and Manchester necessitated frequent speed restrictions.[17]

At the time of writing it is 20 years since these admirable locomotives came into service, and it is likely that their ultimate departure will arouse a nostalgic regret that in 1959 one would never have expected to be associated with a diesel. Bond comments, however, that there was nothing to choose between them and the 'Peaks'.[18]

The 'Peaks', more powerful additions to British Railways' fleet of Type 4s, first arrived in 1959. They also are 1Co-Co1 diesel-electrics. The first 10, originally numbered D1 to D10 and forming what is now Class 44, were built by British Railways at Derby. Their Sulzer engines have of course been described and they have Crompton Parkinson electrical equipment. They were all named after peaks in England and Wales. Their weight of 136 tons is very similar to that of the Class 40s, and they too are excessively long due to their four-axle bogies. They have, however, the advantage of 300 extra horsepower. They were followed by another, and much larger, batch of 127 similar locomotives but with the uprated engine of 2,500hp. These became Class 45. Finally there were 56 more with the same horsepower but with Brush electrical equipment instead of Crompton Parkinson, on account of the easier maintenance of the former. This final batch is Class 46. On their introduction the 'Peaks' had the distinction of being the most powerful single-engined diesel locomotives in the world.[19] The Class 45s all went to the London Midland Region, and they became particularly prominent on the express passenger services of the old Midland Railway main line. The Class 46s are divided between the Western and Eastern Regions.

Many of the 45s and one 46 are named after regiments and corps of the British Army, carrying on a tradition which was started on the London Midland & Scottish Railway in the naming of engines of the 'Royal Scot' and 'Patriot' (or 'Baby Scot') classes. Some of these names have been repeated on the 45s, whilst others have been modified to reflect the amalgamations which have taken place in recent years. For instance, No D551 (later No 45.144) *Royal Signals* bears the name previously carried by 'Patriot' class 4-6-0 No 5504. (At the naming ceremony of No 5504 at Euston, R. A. Riddles was responsible for the appearance of the locomotive, whilst the Author was responsible for the Royal Signals guard of honour). In the postwar amalgamations, The King's Own Royal Regiment (Lancaster) and The Border Regiment

were amalgamated as The King's Own Royal Border Regiment. 'Royal Scot' class No 6161 had been named *The King's Own* and No 6136 *The Border Regiment*. No D58 (later No 45.043) is named *The King's Own Royal Border Regiment*.

The Type 4 locomotives for the Western Region were all diesel-hydraulics. The first were five 'Warship' class, of A1A-A1A wheel arrangement and Voith hydraulic transmission, built by the North British Locomotive Company and named after ships of the Royal Navy. They compared unfavourably with the Swindon built 'Warships' in their weight of 117 tons, as against the latter's modest 79 tons, and none lasted long enough to receive the numerical classification. The British Railways' 'Warships' built at Swindon (later Class 42) were based on the V200 class of the German Federal Railways, but modified to suit the British loading gauge. There were two varieties of Swindon 'Warship'. The first 38 of 1958 had Maybach engines and Mekydro transmission (though one of these later received Paxman engines); whilst the next 33 of 1960 had MAN engines and Voith transmissions and were designated Class 43. Some initial trouble with their bogies led to a temporary reduction in permissible speed; but Bond says that they eventually turned out well.[20] All have now been scrapped owing to the standardisation of electric transmission by British Railways.

The remaining and most powerful class of diesel-hydraulics were the 'Western' or 52 class of 1961. They had Maybach engines but with the Voith transmission, which had shown its superiority over the Mekydro. Their characteristics have been discussed in Chapter 5, and they have performed very well on the principal expresses of the Western Region. There was some trouble at first with the cardan shaft transmission, and Bond says that S.C. Ell did very good work in finding out the cause and curing it.[21] Some at any rate of the Western Region drivers preferred them to the diesel-electrics of equivalent power because of the insurance provided by two engines, rather than one, and on account of their comfortable draught-free cabs. All had names beginning with the word 'Western', so continuing the Great Western tradition of 'Saints', 'Courts', 'Ladies', 'Stars', 'Abbeys', 'Castles', 'Kings', etc. Furthermore, the nameplates were typically Great Western. All have now been withdrawn for the same reason as the 'Warships'.

A year after the 'Westerns' came the first of a new Type 4 diesel-electric class; a development of the 'Peaks'. A locomotive was needed that was lighter than the 'Peaks' and with fewer axles, giving it greater route availability. British Railways stated the requirements for such a locomotive and three different designs were produced to meet it. English Electric built the DP2, the engine of which was discussed in the last chapter and which is mentioned again later. Brush produced their Co-Co No D0280 *Falcon*, powered by two Maybach engines, similar to those of the 'Western' class but with electric transmission. The reason for selecting this engine was that Brush, since 1956, had held the exclusive United Kingdom manufacturing rights for Maybach engines, which were actually made by Bristol-Siddeley; but both companies had been part of the Hawker Siddeley Group since 1957. The design was prepared in consultation with British Railways[22] and the locomotive was completed in September 1961. The name *Falcon* was derived from the Brush Falcon Works at Loughborough, but this was actually the fourth express locomotive in the British Isles to bear the name. The first was a three-cylinder compound 4-4-0 No 84, built in 1932 for the Great Northern Railway (Ireland), to haul the Belfast-Dublin expresses; the second was a London & North Eastern Railway A4 Pacific, the first number of which, by a peculiar coincidence, was No 4484; and the third was No 101, one of a class of diesel-electric locomotives built for Northern Ireland Railways for the Belfast-Dublin service bearing the bird names of their steam predecessors.

After successful trials No D0280 went to the Western Region (doubtless on account of its Maybach engines) and was allotted the class designation of 53.

A third locomotive, No D0260 *Lion*, was built by the Birmingham Railway Carriage & Wagon Company in conjunction with Associated Electrical Industries and Sulzer Brothers. It was powered by a new version of the Sulzer engine employed in the 'Peaks' and had AEI electrical equipment. British Railways in due course invited Brush to submit suitable design studies incorporating Brush electrical equipment but embodying *Lion's* Sulzer engine.

In October 1962 Brush delivered No D1500 to British Railways, the first of what was to be Class 47, and an initial batch of 20 were completed by March 1963. Further orders followed and Brush eventually built 310, whilst a further 202 were constructed at Crewe. They formed the largest group of general-purpose locomotives in Europe.[23]

Trials with a locomotive of this class have been described in Chapter 5. In spite of the engine troubles mentioned in the last chapter, the 47s have been most successful, and have hauled the bulk of express passenger and many freight trains all over the British Railways system. Class 47 has been chosen as one of those to last into the 1990s, and, as one of them has been given an English Electric 16RK3CT engine of 3,250hp, it may be intended to re-engine all of them to obtain more power.[24]

A number of the 47s allocated to the Western Region were given names, at the instance of the late R. F. Hanks, when he was Chairman of the Western Area Board.[25] Many of these names were originally borne by Great Western broad gauge engines, but three eminent Great Western engineers are appropriately honoured: Isambard Kingdon Brunel, Sir Daniel Gooch, and George Jackson Churchward. Hanks once said to the Author that he wondered what that great steam engineer, Churchward, would have thought of diesel motive power.

The last of the Type 4 locomotives are those comprising Class 50; their origin lay in the very successful trial locomotive DP2. R. C. Bond says that the design and manufacture of the DP2 was due to the existence in English Electric of two rival factions; of which one favoured and produced the 'Deltic', with its two high speed two-stroke engines, whilst the other heartily disliked the 'Deltic' design, and their preference for a medium speed engine resulted in the construction of DP2. Bond

adds that this was the best diesel locomotive running on British Railways, till it was destroyed in an accident.[26]

The success of DP2 led to the construction by English Electric of 50 locomotives of basically similar design, to be leased to British Railways, though remaining English Electric property. Originally the D400 class, they were later Class 50, and some time later ownership passed to British Railways.

The trouble experienced with the engine of these locomotives has already been discussed; but unfortunately this was not the only trouble that beset them. Due, apparently, to difficulties experienced over delayed action by the rheostatic brakes on the AL6 (later Class 86) electric locomotives, British Railways decided that a more sophisticated control system was desirable. Prototype control equipments incorporating thyristors were designed by English Electric and fitted to three 25kV ac multiple-units operating, respectively, on London Midland, Eastern, and Scottish Regions. As a result of trials with these units, British Railways asked that a development of this advanced electronic equipment should be incorporated in the D400.[27] The decision was premature and unfortunate, for the locomotives suffered from what R.G. Jarvis has called 'a too early application of too much electronics.[28]

The Class 50s were first employed to operate the London-Glasgow expresses north of Crewe, whilst electric haulage terminated there; a task that they performed very well in spite of their troubles. After the completion of electrification to Glasgow, most of them were transferred to the Western Region in replacement of the 'Western' class. Now that their 'teething' problems have been surmounted they have proved very good locomotives, and have indeed entered British Railways' elite because all of them have been named. Like the 'Warship' classes, they are named after ships of the Royal Navy, and many of the names previously borne by the former have been repeated.

There was a curious sequel to this story, in that in 1968 the Portuguese Railways ordered 10 locomotives similar to DP2, firmly rejecting offers to incorporate the 'refinements' introduced in the Class 50![29]

Type 5

The earliest, and for a long time the only, Class 5 locomotives were the 'Deltics'. The successful trials with the prototype are described in Chapter 3. The production locomotives have done magnificent work on the East Coast route, and were the only locomotives available that could have worked the principal expresses on the fast schedules that their arrival permitted. They were expensive to maintain, but R. C. Bond says that the expense was not excessive in relation to their performance.[30] They were not ordered by the London Midland Region because the decision had been taken to electrify at last the southern portion of the West Coast route.[31] Continuing a LNER tradition, some of these 22 locomotives were named after race horses and others after regiments of the British Army.

The last of the Type 5 locomotives at the time of writing are those of Class 56 ordered by British Railways in 1974. They are intended for heavy freight and mark a divergence from the policy adopted by British Railways of building general-purpose locomotives, to one of working passenger services with either multiple-unit trains or train sets with power cars, and providing locomotives only for freight. British Railways wanted 60 of the Class 56, of which 30 were to be built by British Rail Engineering Limited and 30 by Brush. However, Brush could not build 30 locomotives of this size in the time required, and so sub-contracted to the Roumanian firm of Electroputers. All the electrical equipment is by Brush. The locomotives built in Roumania had sundry faults, so that in fact no time was saved by ordering abroad.[32] Subsequently BREL built another 30, so that by the end of 1978 the fleet numbered 90 locomotives.

The High Speed Trains were all built by BREL, but the electrical equipment was provided by Brush, so that this firm now takes a very prominent place in the construction of the mechanical parts and electrical equipment of diesel-electric locomotives.

The advent of diesel traction on systems which had been previously operated by steam locomotives entailed a complete change in maintenance methods. Steam engines need running sheds, where maintenance is carried out, whereas diesels only require a 'home'. The ideal steam running shed was the 'through' type, in which locomotives came in at one end, had the necessary maintenance work done, and eventually passed out at the other end. Some steam sheds were 'dead end'; that is, with no exit from the far, or back, end; and difficulties arose when engines had been repaired and had to be got out from the back.[33]

All diesel locomotive maintenance is controlled from a centralised office. On the London Midland Region this is at Crewe, whilst on other Regions it is done from traffic control offices. All the old running sheds were replaced by a very much smaller number of maintenance depots, to which locomotives go when they are due for maintenance. Each diesel locomotive has a home depot where a detailed record of its maintenance is kept. All maintenance is not necessarily carried out at the home depot, but if done at another depot it has to be reported to the home depot.[34]

For maintenance on the Great Eastern line Miller produced a design for a diesel depot which was adopted subsequently throughout British Railways. In essence, two 'dead end' sheds were arranged back to back with the repair facilities between them. A locomotive coming in for maintenance could either run straight into one of these sheds, or run past both and reverse into the far one.[35]

Diesel maintenance requires a high standard of cleanliness. Any cleaning cloths giving off 'fluff' had to be banned, and they were replaced by launderers' rags, mainly from women's underwear. Air filters need special cleaning and a filter cleaning room was established in every depot. Filters are treated with an oily adhesive into which they are dipped. Engine oil is subjected to spectographic analysis. (Oil burned in front of a spectograph shows what minerals are present, and thus whether components are breaking down.) This is an important insurance against failure. In winter the only satisfactory insurance against engines seizing up is to keep them running. Anti-freeze is too expensive and, in any case, if used

in the quantities needed, it could cause damage. Train heating boilers presented the most troublesome maintenance problem. The controls are fragile and will not stand up to vibration; it is a problem that has never really been solved.[36]

Space does not permit too much attention to diesel railcars. There are a very large number, mostly with the underfloor 'bus' type engine and mechanical drive, and built by Derby Works, Swindon Works, Metropolitan-Cammell, Gloucester Railway Carriage & Wagon Co, Birmingham Railway Carriage & Wagon Co, Cravens, Park Royal, and the Pressed Steel Co. R. G. Jarvis says that he started in 1937 as a protagonist for the underfloor 'bus' engine, but later when he went to the Southern Region, who had chosen an English Electric design with medium speed above-floor engine and electric transmission, he became convinced that his was the best solution.[37] Miller agrees with him and thinks the underfloor 'bus' engine poor.[38] The intention that the new Class 210 multiple-units should be diesel-electric with an above-floor high speed engine was mentioned in the last chapter. This may, therefore, be the pattern for the future.

NOTES

1 Bond, R. C.; Information to the Author
2 Carter, R. S.; *British Railways Main Line Diesels;* Ian Allan Ltd, 1963, p36, Webb, Brian; *The English Electric Main Line Diesels of British Rail;* David & Charles, 1976, p32-8; GEC Traction Ltd, *1,000hp Diesel-Electric Locomotives for British Rail*
3 Bond, op cit
4 Miller, T. C. B.; Information to the Author
5 ibid
6 Webb, Brian; *Sulzer Diesel Locomotives of British Rail;* David & Charles, 1978, pp22-3
7 ibid, p19
8 ibid, pp23-5
9 Bond, op cit
10 ibid
11 Miller, op cit
12 Bond, op cit
13 Webb, *English Electric,* pp61-2
14 Carter, op cit, p32
15 Bond, op cit
16 Webb, *English Electric,* op cit, p48
17 Carter, op cit, p6
18 Bond, op cit
19 Walker, Julian A.; *BR-Sulzer Class 44, 45, 46;* Diesel & Electric Group and D. Bradford Barton, 1976, p16
20 Bond, op cit
21 Bond, op cit
22 Toms, George; *Brush Diesel Locomotives 1940-78;* Turntable Publications, 1978, p44
23 ibid, p60
24 Ringer, Brian; *Brush-Sulzer Class 47;* Diesel & Electric Group and D. Bradford Barton, p22
25 Rogers, Colonel H. C. B.; *G. J. Churchward, A Locomotive Biography;* George Allen & Unwin, 1975, p172
26 Bond, op cit
27 GEC Traction Ltd, *2700hp Diesel-Electrics for British Rail.* Institution of Electrical Engineers, *Conference on Performance of Electrified Railways,* October 1968; A. H. Emerson, 'Main Line 25kV 50 Hz AC Electrification on

London Midland Region of British Rail', p142; IEE op cit,
C. M. S. Maguire, 'The Suburban Aspects of British Rail
25kV AC Electrification', p172

28 Jarvis, R. G.; Information to the Author
29 GEC Traction Ltd, Information to the Author
30 Bond, op cit
31 ibid
32 Toms, op cit, p100
33 Miller, op cit
34 ibid
35 ibid
36 ibid
37 Jarvis op cit
38 Miller, op cit

Below: The English Electric Type 1s only make appearances on passenger trains during the summer, such as Nos 20. 134 and 20.039 at Nottingham on a Skegness-Derby holiday train in July 1979./*A. Wynn*

Bottom: Two Clayton Type 1s run light at Ribblehead in August, 1963, en route to the Scottish Region for entry into service./*A.W. Martin*

Right: Clayton Type 1s in production during 1962 at the manufacturer's Derby works./*Railway Industry Association*

Bottom right: The North British Type 1./*GEC*

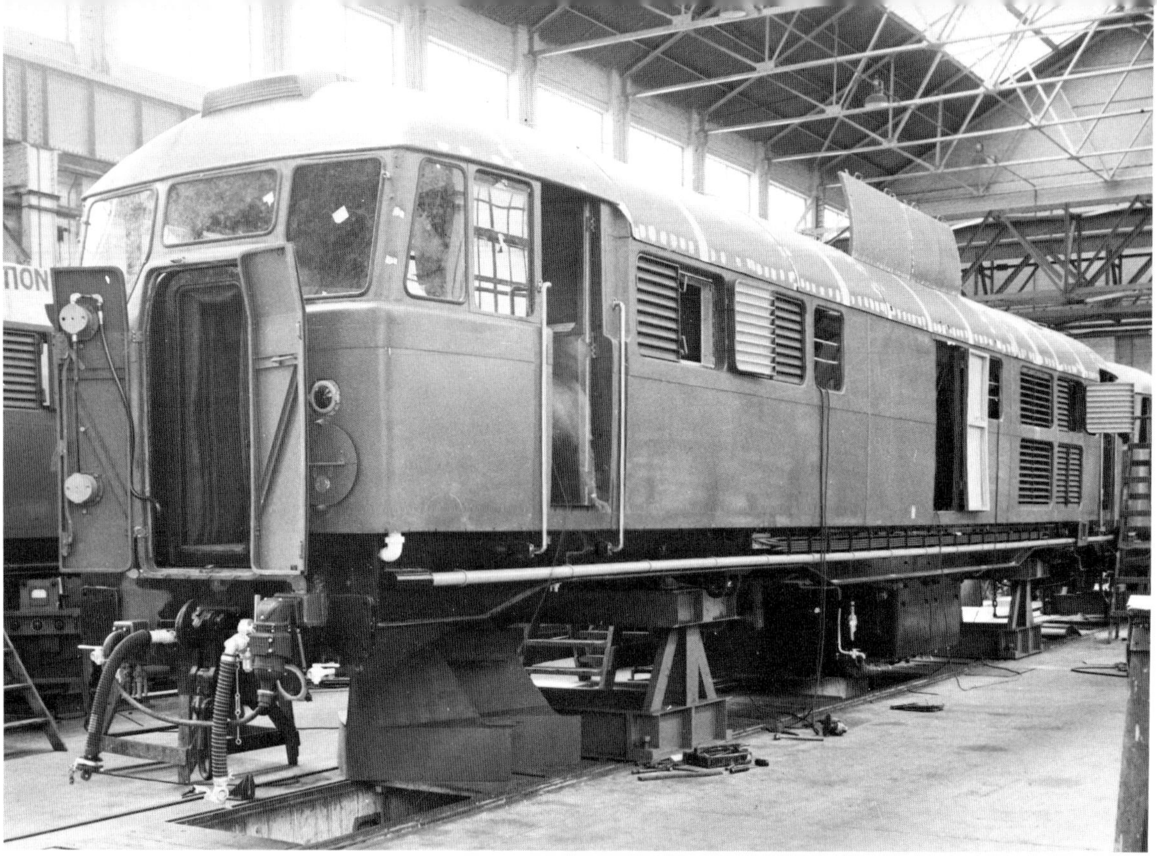

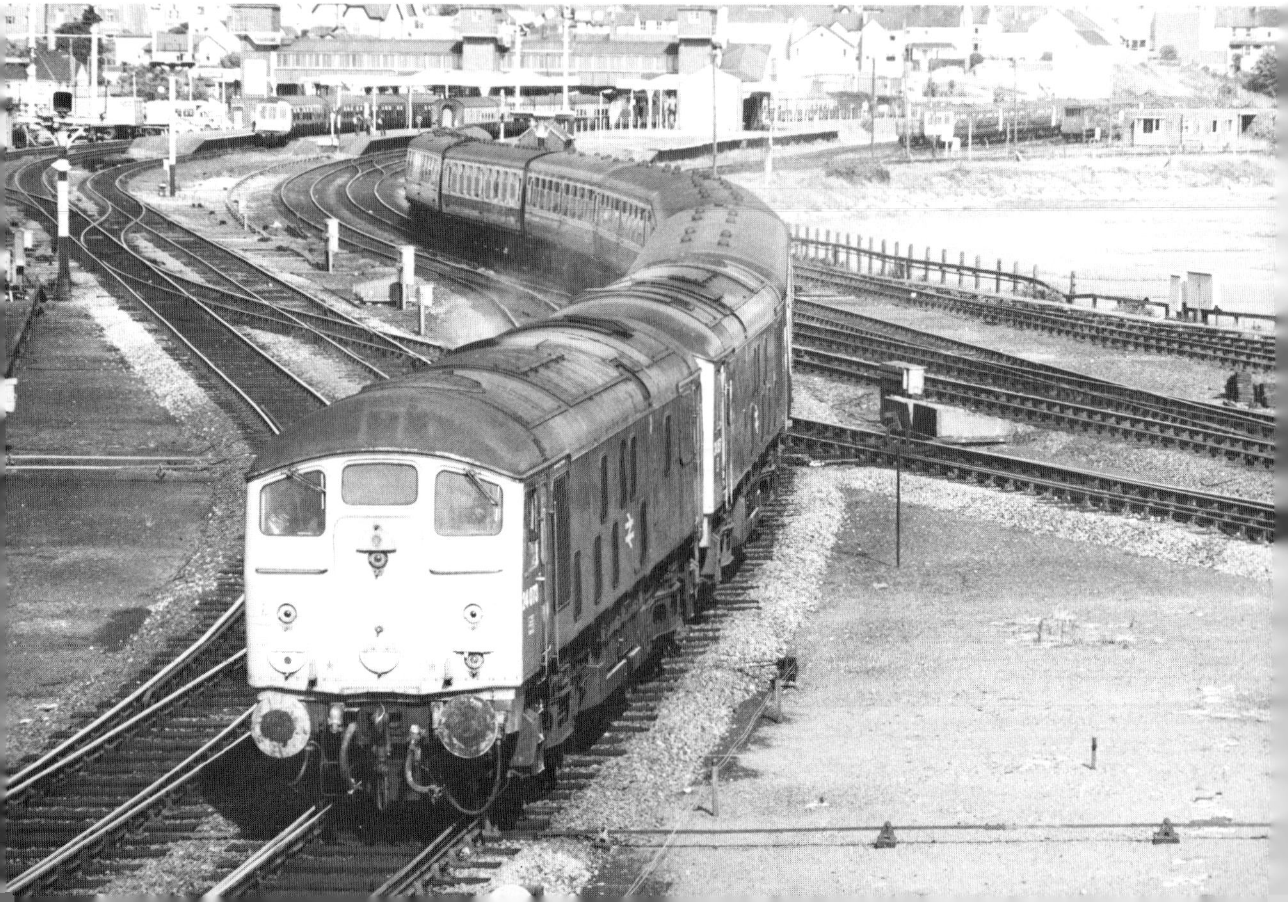

Above left: An early Brush Type 2 takes shape at Loughborough./*Brush*

Left: The BR/Sulzer Type 2. Two of them, No 24.073 leading, take the Llandudno line out of the Junction with empty stock in 1977, in the evening of their days./*Larry Goddard*

Above: Class 26 No 26.027 at Helmsdale on an Inverness-Wick-Thurso train in May 1977. /*Brian E. Morrison*

Centre right: 'Baby Deltic' No 5902 on a GN main line stopping train, soon after introduction in 1959./*GEC*

Below right: North British Type 2 No D6335 on a test train somewhere on the Scottish Region./*Railway Industry Association*

The BRCW Type 3 locomotives for the Southern Region at work as Class 33. *Top:* No 33.005 breasts the climb out of Buckhorn Weston Tunnel on an Exeter-Waterloo express in May 1978. *Above:* No 33.104 propels a Weymouth-Waterloo train at Dorchester in August 1978./*G.F. Gillham; John Scrace*

Top right: Class 33s on parade at Hither Green./*R.I. Wallace*

Right: Now designated Class 37, No D6999 poses for a publicity event in 1965 in South Wales./*GEC*

33040

5T17
THE 300TH
ENGLISH ELECTRIC
STANDARD TYPE 3 DIESEL ELECTRIC LOCOMOTIVE
FOR BRITISH RAILWAYS

Above: Class 37s on one of their 'star turns' of the mid to late 1970s, haulage of the Port Talbot-Llanwen ore trains. Nos 37.307/305/ 301 at Bridgend, headed east./*J. A. Phillips*

Left: 'Hymek' No D7000 in all its ex-works finery at Beyer Peacock's Gorton Works on 3 May 1961./*Sam Lambert*

Above right: D200 heyday. The first of the class at the head of a special press trip from Liverpool St-Norwich on 18 April 1958 seen just east of Colchester./*BR*

Right: Present day D200 now designated Class 40. No 40.112 in the repair shop at BREL Crewe works./*L.P. Gater*

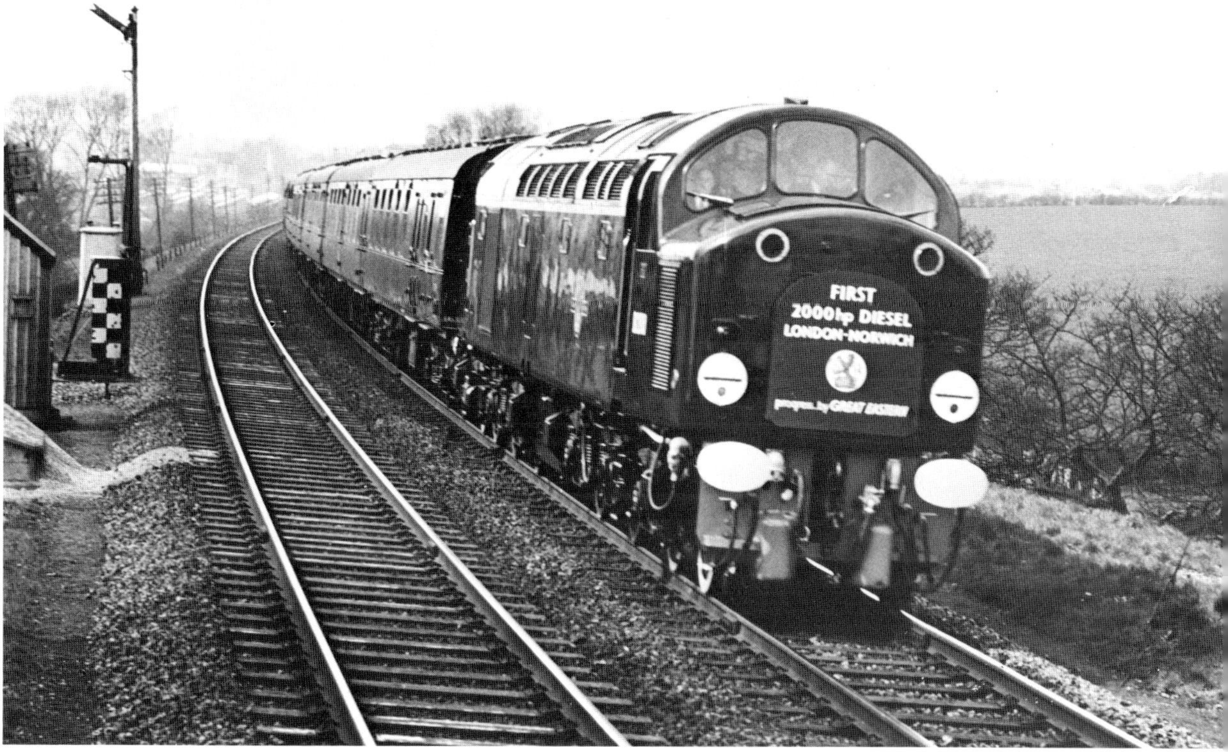
FIRST
2000 hp DIESEL
LONDON-NORWICH

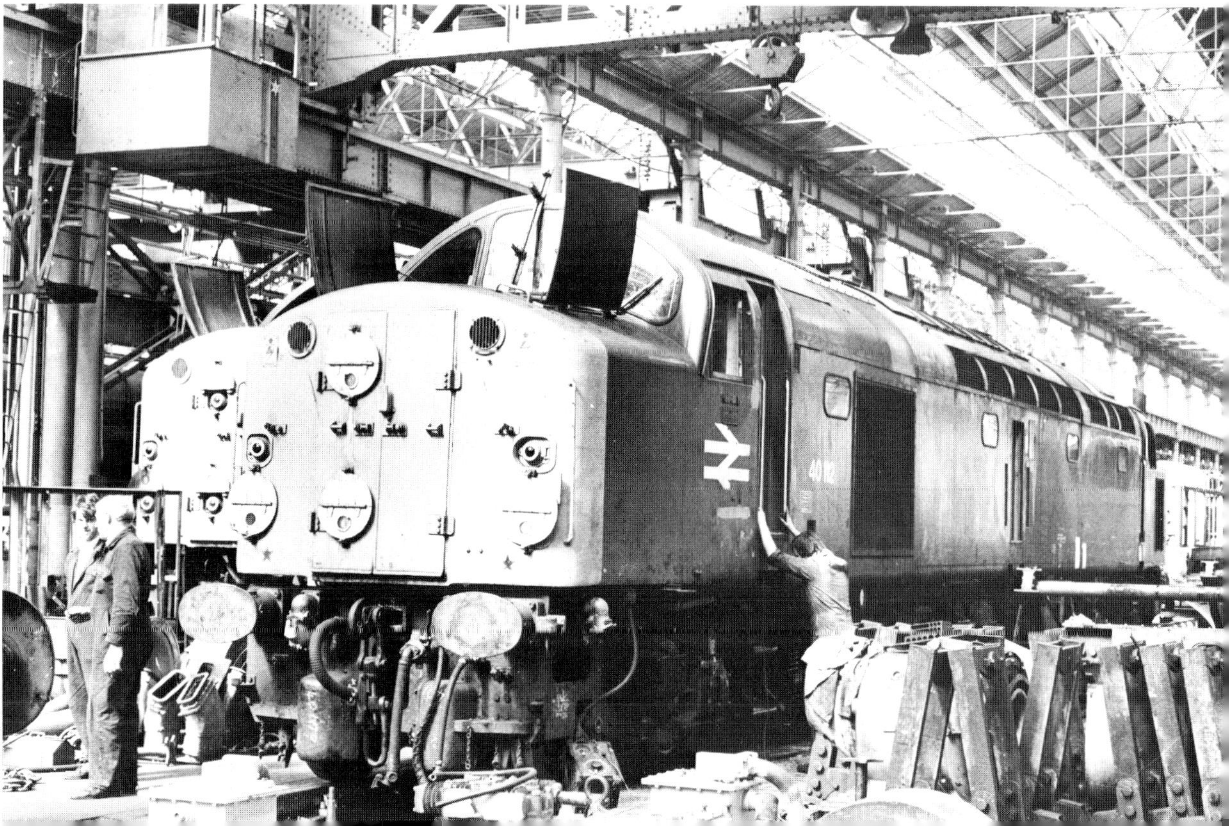

Top: Class 46 No 46.041 on the Settle & Carlisle main line in June 1979, heading a Nottingham-Carlisle semi-fast./*Colin J. Marsden*

Above: North British Type 4 No D603 *Conquest* on arrival at Paddington in August 1960, at the head of an up Penzance express. /*Dennis C. Ovenden*

Top right: The Brush *Falcon* on test in its early days./*Brush*

Right: The Brush Type 4 design made a grand impression on Eastern Region GN Line, 7 class freights. No D1511 takes a down Ferme Park-New England 7 past Welwyn North in October 1963./*Brian Stephenson*

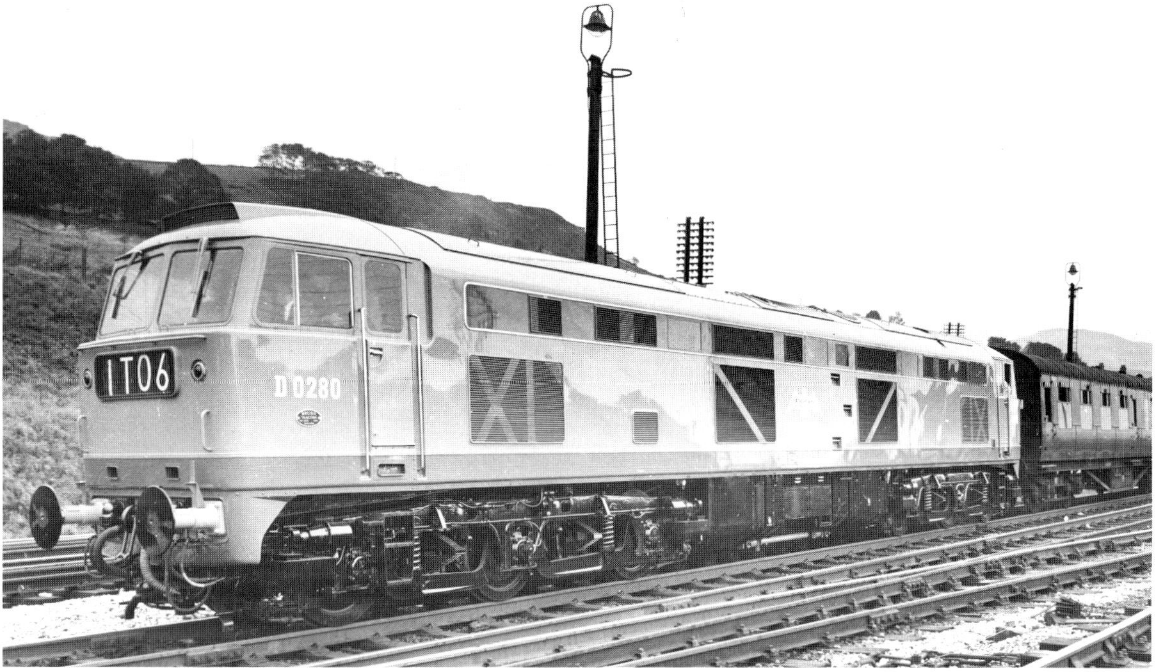
1T06
D 0280

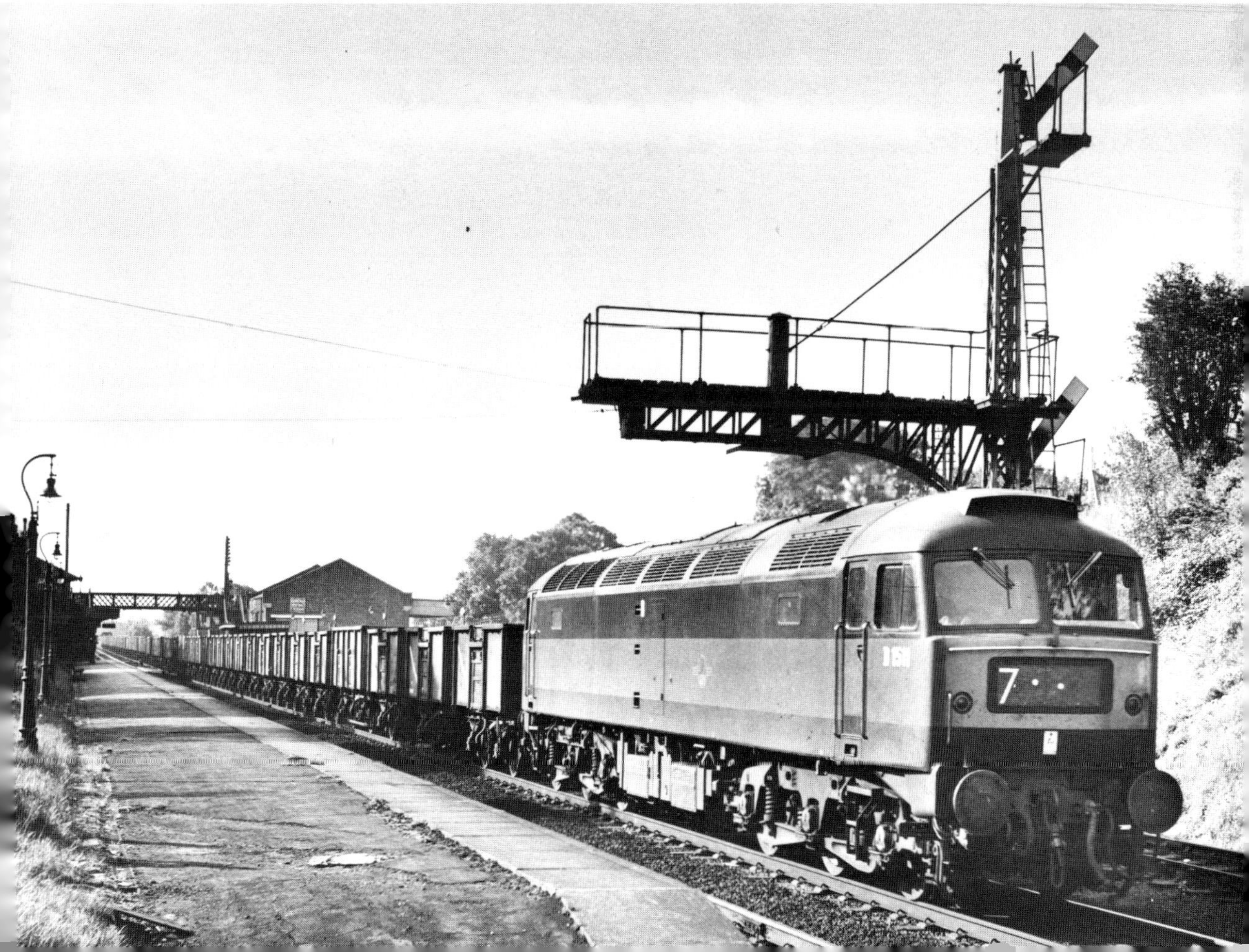

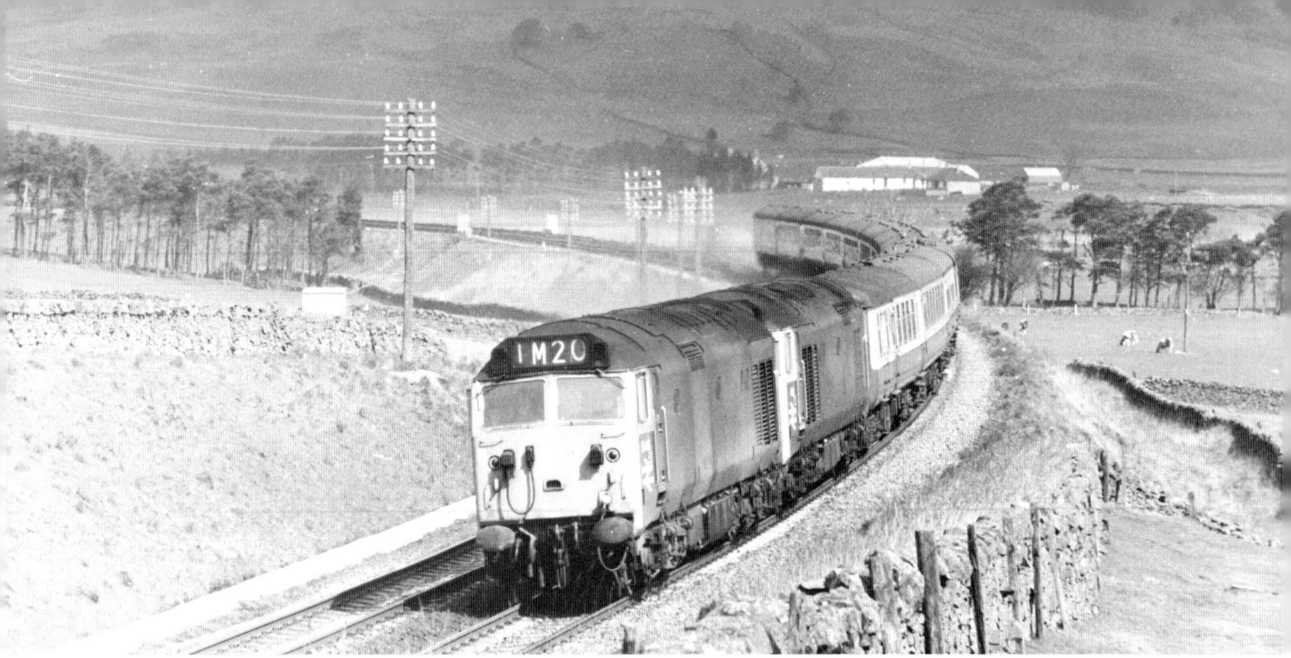
1M20

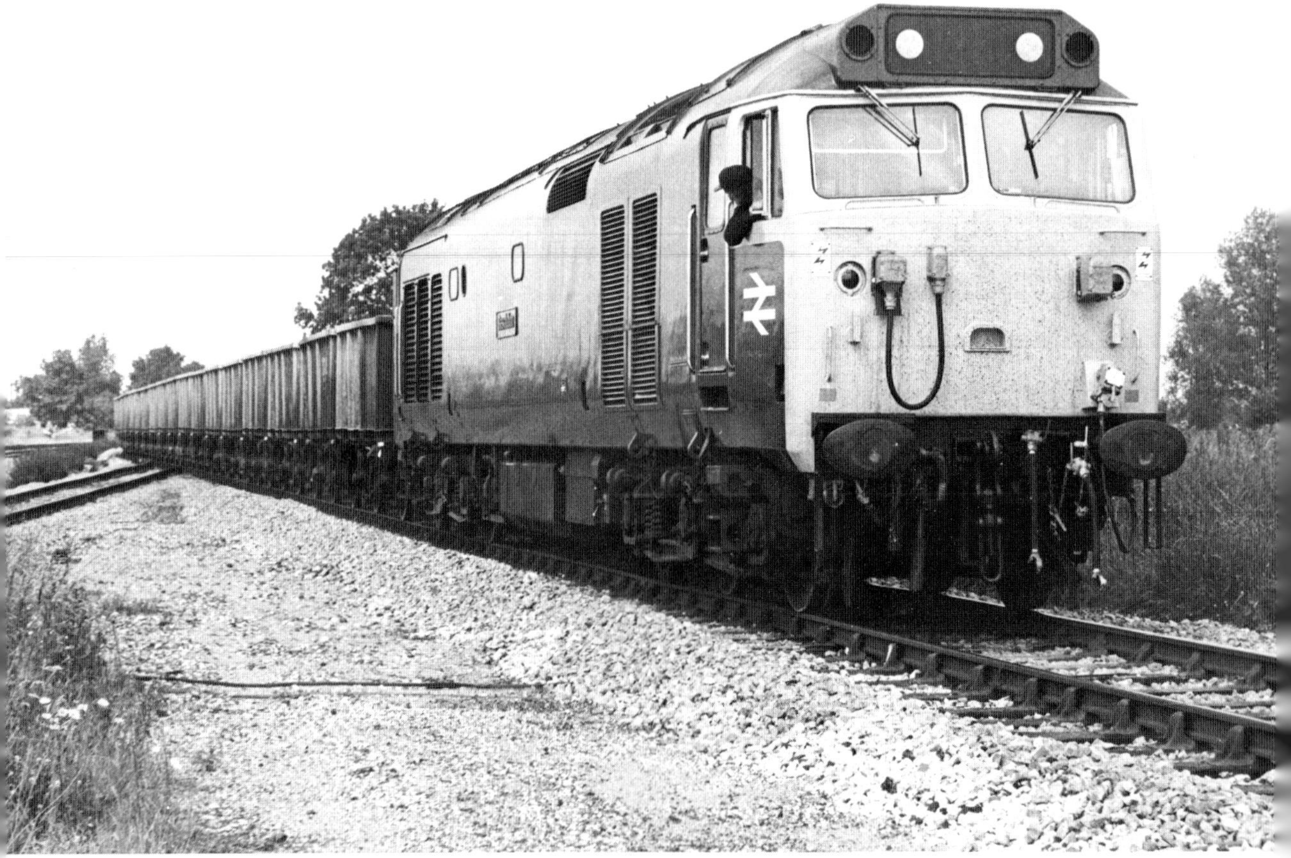

Top left: Two Class 50s, Nos 446 and 418, in the Clyde Valley, near Crawford, with the up 'Royal Scot' in 1971./*J. H. Cooper-Smith*

Left. Different duties for a Class 50 on the Western Region. Now named *Resolution,* No 50.018 backs up the loop at Aldermaston, waiting to leave with a Westbury stone empties train in July 1979./*D.E. Canning*

A comparison of diesel traction maintenance depot styles. *Top:* The 'repair Works' principle adopted by the Western Region only. This example is Cardiff Canton. This late 1964 shot shows the four types that did battle in the 1965 electric v hydraulic appraisal. *Above:* The Scottish Region's Eastfield depot, Glasgow in 1977./*BR; L.A. Nixon*

Right: Difficult to resist including this March 1959 industrial designer's proposal for the external styling of the production 'Deltics'. /*Sam Lambert*

Below: Typical 'Deltic' – the engines are opened up and exhaust shoots skyward on D9000, still un-named and with flashing headlight fitted, at Finsbury Park depot in March 1961. /*Sam Lambert*

Bottom: One of the Southern Region's diesel-electric 3-car Hampshire units, No 1118, nears Fareham on a Southampton-Portsmouth working in April 1960./*J.C. Haydon*

9
Electrification

Most railway mechanical engineers would probably agree that electric traction provides the ideal motive power. Its disadvantage is the high capital cost of installation; so that it has been generally confined to routes on which the traffic is sufficiently dense to recover this cost within a reasonable time, or on which, as compared with other modes, it offers particular advantages.

The benefits of electrification are considerable. The maintenance of electric locomotives is much cheaper than that of diesel locomotives, because they do not carry their own power plant; and for the same reason electric locomotives are less prone to failure and have a life expectancy of about 30 years or more, as compared with some 20 years for diesels. Electricity can be supplied to the conductors by power stations fed by coal, oil, atomic fuel, or water power; whereas diesel traction depends entirely on oil.

Comparatively cheap oil fuel provided the impetus behind the rapid scrapping of steam power in favour of diesel; but some 20 years later the dwindling stocks of the world's oil and its consequent rapidly rising cost make electrification much the more attractive proposition.

On British Railways 45% of all train-miles are now electrically operated, though this is over only 20% of the total route-mileage.[1] But BR have been requested by the Government to submit proposals for a wide programme of electrification, and the Chairman of BR, Sir Peter Parker, has said: 'What we are hoping to do is to explore the case for a rolling programme of core main line electrification over perhaps 20 years — embracing anything up to 3,000 miles of inter-city routes — and we are working towards this objective now.'[2] Proposals for the next 10 years cover the extension of existing electrified routes to displace the maximum number of diesel locomotives, a cross-London link with connections to four Regions, and certain suburban schemes.[3]

Many will consider that present developments fully justify Riddles' advocacy of electrification in 1951 (as recorded in Chapter 1). Had that advice been followed, it is possible that both the East Coast route and the Western Region routes to Plymouth and South Wales would have been electrified by now, with immense savings in capital costs. As it is, the present and future electrifications in Great Britain are due primarily to the vision of two men: Sir Herbert Walker, General Manager of the Southern Railway; and Robert Riddles, former Vice-President of the LMS and later Member for Mechanical and Electrical Engineering on the Railway Executive.

Electric traction is of course a far older system of motive power than diesel, though paradoxically it is increasingly presenting itself as the successor to the latter.

Probably the first commercial electric railway in the British Isles was that running alongside the road from Portrush to Bushmills in County Antrim, and eventually to the Giant's Causeway. Power to make the line had been obtained in 1880 by two brothers, and one of them, W. A. Traill, who was engineer of the line, drew the attention of Dr William Siemens, of the famous electrical firm, to its suitability for electrification on account of the water power available at Bushmills. On 28 September 1883 the line was officially opened by the Lord Lieutenant of Ireland, though there were electric excursions for fare-paying passengers in the previous June and July. Electrification was initially on the third-rail system with direct current at 250 volts supplied by the hydro-electric plant at Bushmills. At the opening ceremony Sir William Thompson (later Lord Kelvin), one of the shareholders, demonstrated the safety of the 250 volt supply by grasping an unearthed terminal with one hand and shaking the hands of unsuspecting guests with the other![4]

It was not long before other electrifications were put in hand. In 1890 the City & London Railway opened, the first electric tube railway in the world. Its trains were hauled by diminutive locomotives which took current at 500 volts from a third-rail situated between the running rails, and had their traction motor armatures built directly on to the running axles. It was the start of London's vast network of tube railways, the construction of which has not finished yet.

In 1893 the Liverpool Overhead Railway was opened, running for 5.5 miles along the docks and the first elevated electric railway in the world. It too was supplied from a third-rail carrying 500V dc. It was followed the next year by the Manx Electric Railway, 18 miles long and of 3ft gauge. It was another 500V dc system, but the current was collected from an overhead conductor wire.

In 1898 the Waterloo & City Railway began operations between Waterloo and the Bank of England. It was the first tube railway to use motorcoaches instead of locomotives. The London & South Western Railway supported the construction of the line, and on 1 January 1907 it acquired it. The third-rail system was used with return through the running rails.

The electrification of the Metropolitan and the Metropolitan District Railways differed from the tubes in that electricity took over from steam. In 1900 an experimental length of track was electrified on the third-rail system between High Street Kensington and Earls Court. This was a joint District and Metropolitan venture. Electrification of both railways was soon to follow, but it was essential that both should adopt the same method.

The Metropolitan wanted a three-phase ac system produced by the Budapest company of Ganz, whereas the District preferred 600V dc with two conductor rails, 'live' and return. The latter system won and this became the standard for the whole of London's Underground network, both tube and 'cut-and-cover'. Multiple-unit trains also became standard, except for those trains which were handed over to steam traction at the end of the electrified tracks of the Metropolitan, and the through workings from the Great Western Railway to the City. These trains were hauled by electric locomotives, which ultimately were the attractive batch of 20 built by Metropolitan-Vickers in 1921-3 and all eventually named after celebrities associated with 'Metroland' and the City.

Although they started their experiments earlier, the District and Metropolitan were beaten in time by the Mersey Railway as being the first urban underground line to change from steam to electric traction; for the latter completed its third- and fourth-rail 650V dc electrification in 1903.

Electrification of urban and suburban railways was hurried along by the construction of electric tramways from about the turn of the century. In the Newcastle area the North Eastern Railway lost a large proportion of its local passengers to the City's trams and to the Tyneside Tramways which served Gosforth, Wallsend and North Shields. In March 1904, therefore, the NER electrified the first section of its Tyneside lines, reaching the coast the following July. The service was operated by multiple-unit trains taking 600V from the third rail. In that same month on the other side of the country the Lancashire & Yorkshire Railway electrified its Liverpool-Southport coast line on the same system but with supply at 630V. Further electrification in this area followed.

The Midland was the next of the main line railways to electrify a section of its lines. In April 1908 the line from Lancaster through Morecambe to Heysham was converted, but the Midland chose 6,600V ac, with overhead collection. It will be recalled that it was on this route that Riddles introduced 50-cycle (now described as 50 Herz) ac to the United Kingdom.

In 1909 the London Brighton & South Coast Railway, which had been badly hit by competition from the London County Council Tramways, completed the electrification of their South London line; copying the Midland by using 6,600V ac overhead supply. In 1911 the LBSCR electrified route was extended via Clapham Junction and Crystal Palace to Selhurst, and the last of the company's lines to be electrified on this system was completed two years after Grouping, in 1925. The standard unit for later LBSCR electrifications consisted of five vehicles. The centre vehicle was a motor van (known as a 'milk van') which was really a Bo-Bo locomotive with two bow collectors. On each side of this were two trailer coaches, the outer ones being driving trailers.

The next interesting development was the production in 1914 by the Darlington Works of the NER of 10 Bo-Bo 1,100hp electric locomotives, designed by Sir Vincent Raven to work the 18-mile long Shildon-Newport line. The electrification of this line at 1,500V dc with overhead collection was completed in 1916. Raven followed these

locomotives in 1922 with a high speed 1,800hp 2-Co-2 locomotive to work express trains over the proposed electrified York-Newcastle main line. It was tested on the Shildon-Newport line, and a photograph shows it hauling 17 bogie coaches. Sadly, the main line electrification never took place, and falling traffic led in 1935 to the Sheldon-Newport line reverting to steam operation.

In 1914 the London & North Western Railway electrified the route from Willesden to Earls Court, and I remember my pleased astonishment in 1919 at seeing a LNWR electric multiple-unit train, in all the glory of purple, brown and spilt milk, standing in Earls Court underground station. In July 1922 the LNWR electric trains began running between Watford and both Euston and Broad Street.

In 1915 the London & South Western Railway opened between Waterloo and Wimbledon through East Putney the first section of a system of electrification that was destined to spread all over the South of England, with a third-rail supplying current at 600V dc.

A year later the Manchester-Bury line of the Lancashire & Yorkshire Railway was electrified on a system that has caused many Southern electrical engineers to regret that it was not chosen for their own railway. Supply was by third-rail, but pick up was by side contact instead of from the top of the rail, and the current was at the high dc voltage of 1,200. The conductor rail had a wood guarding to prevent accidental contact. The advantages of the system were that there were fewer sub-stations than with 600V dc and there was virtual immunity from icing.

In 1932 the Manchester South Junction & Altrincham Railway (a joint LMS and LNER line) was electrified at 1,500V dc with overhead collection. This was in accordance with the Weir Report to the Minister of Transport in 1927 on the future system of electrification in the United Kingdom, and the MSJ&A was the first railway to follow the recommendations.

The last electrification completed in Great Britain before the 1939-45 war was the conversion of the LMS lines in the Wirral Peninsula. This project included the running of trains into Liverpool Central via the Mersey Railway, which tunnels under the River Mersey. The Mersey Railway's 650V dc supply with conductor rail was therefore adopted.

Southern

On 1 January 1912 Sir (as he later became) Herbert Walker took up the appointment of General Manager of the London & South Western Railway. He was faced immediately with the problem of halting the fall in passenger traffic on the LSWR suburban line. Against the competition by the trams and the threatened expansion of the tube railways, the only solution was electrification. Walker and H.W. Jones, the electrical engineer of the LSWR's Waterloo & City Railway, favoured third-rail collection at 600V dc, which had already shown itself to be technically reliable and commercially profitable. They did not like the LBSC overhead ac system, for although it was commercially successful, it suffered from the weakness of the 25Hz commutator motor, and the overhead array was very rigid, slow to construct, and very expensive. A conductor rail, on the other hand, was cheap and simple to install, and 25Hz rotary convertor substations to feed the dc traction motors were a proved and satisfactory combination. The choice of such a system, indeed, was justified in the light of technical knowledge and experience at the time.[5] As regards relative speed of construction, the LSWR had 47 miles of electric route by 1916, three years after work had started, whereas the LBSCR took five years to electrify 47 miles of single track.[6] It was inevitable, therefore, that when the Southern Railway was formed in 1923 the LSWR system should be selected for the new company. The LBSCR overhead electrification was abandoned in 1930.

Passenger trains formed the bulk of the Southern services and it was decided that multiple-unit traction would provide the best method of operation. The advantages were rapid acceleration, operating flexibility, easy alteration of train make-up, short turn-round of trains in congested terminals, and current collection shoes distributed down the train which ensured continued current supply at conductor rail gaps.[7]

The Southern objective was the electrification of its whole system, except for those lines on which traffic was insufficiently heavy to make the cost worthwhile. This policy was continued after Nationalisation, and with the electrification to the Kentish coast and to Bournemouth the aim was virtually achieved.

Before 1963 most multiple-unit sets were either two-coach or four-coach; the basic type consisting of a motor coach with two motors and a trailing coach. From 1963, however, standard four-coach units have contained one four-motor coach and have driving trailers at each end. The electrification to Bournemouth, on account of the non-electrified continuation to Weymouth, brought the train make-up described in the last chapter. This was the first push-pull operation of high-speed trains to be introduced into the United Kingdom, the normal maximum operating speed being 90mile/h.[8]

The Southern has not been a great user of electric locomotives for the reasons stated above, but they are needed for working special coaching stock and freight trains. The first three locomotives were built by the Southern Railway and had English Electric equipment, including six 245hp nose-suspended traction motors and a motor generator booster set which enabled the locomotives to keep moving over gaps on the conductor rails. English Electric delivered the equipment in 1939, but the war held up construction and they were put into service in 1941, 1943, and 1948 respectively. The wheel arrangement was Co-Co. They were used primarily on the old LBSCR routes, and indeed the first British main line express train to be hauled regularly by an electric locomotive was the Newhaven boat train, which was worked by them from 1948. They were still at work on the Central Division in 1968 but have all now been withdrawn.

In 1958 the first of the 24 Bo-Bo locomotives of 2,552hp were built. They had English Electric equipment, including a motor generator booster set, and SLM flexible drive. Most of their work was on the 'Golden Arrow'

express and the 'Night Ferry'. Later they became Class 71.

In 1962 R. G. Jarvis became Mechanical Engineer, Design, on the Southern Region and, in addition to his responsibility for the drawing offices at Brighton, Eastleigh and Ashford, he took over the carriage and wagon drawing offices as well. He kept this appointment until he was transferred to Derby in the corresponding position in 1964. It was during his time with the Southern that Jarvis designed the remarkable Class 73 electro-diesel locomotives. He says that they were most useful and successful and 'must have been the most versatile locomotives ever built'.[9] They were of Bo-Bo type with four English Electric 400hp traction motors and an English Electric 4-cylinder 4SRKT Mark II 600hp diesel engine. They could thus work either direct from a 750V dc supply from the third-rail, or, when this was not available, with the diesel generator powering the traction motors. The purpose of the design was to make the greatest possible use of the fixed equipment by using electric power when on an electrified track, while enabling the locomotives to produce a high tractive effort in sidings and on other non-electrified track, where only moderate speeds were necessary.[10] Maximum speed with electric power is 90 mile/h. The first Class 73s were turned out in 1962 and they eventually numbered 48.

Subsequently 10 of the Class 71 were converted to electro-diesels for the Southampton boat trains, and became Class 74. Both Classes 71 and 74 have now been withdrawn, because the 'Golden Arrow' has gone, the Southampton boat trains are almost non-existent, and the 'Night Ferry' loading, which could formerly reach 720 tons, has been sufficiently reduced to be within the capacity of the 73s. The freight Ferry trains are now worked either by 73s or 33s. Jarvis says that 'the 74s, like the 50s, suffered from a too early application of too much electronics'.[11]

The advisability of retaining the low-voltage system on the Southern was reviewed at various times. In June 1956 the Ministry of Transport gave formal approval to the British Transport Commission's report in favour of 25kV ac as the future standard for electrification of British Railways; whilst at the same time accepting the Commission's recommendation that the Southern Region should complete its own electrification on the third-rail system. However, it was considered advisable that the preliminary estimates for the extension of electrification to Bournemouth should contain comparisons of the respective costs of 25kV ac, 1,500V dc, third-rail, 750V dc, third-rail, and diesel. The attraction of a 1,500V conductor rail supply was due, of course to the success of the Manchester-Bury line's 1,200V dc with side collection from a protected third-rail, allowing a reduction in number of substations and giving freedom from icing. However, the savings produced by halving the number of substations was unfortunately more than offset by the cost of the additional rolling stock. Conversion of the third-rail system between Waterloo and Brookwood to overhead collection was considered impracticable because the closely spaced tracks on viaduct for more than three miles between Waterloo and Clapham Junction, carrying exceptionally heavy traffic, would have made it prohibitively expensive, apart from the difficulties of operating two different systems side by side. Extending the existing third-rail system by an overhead route was also examined and discarded, and diesel operation offered no alternative solution.[12]

Manchester-Sheffield-Wath

The first complete scheme for electrifying the Manchester-Sheffield lines, at 1,500V dc with overhead supply, was worked out in detail by the London & North Eastern Railway in 1926. Nothing was done at the time for various reasons, but in 1936 fresh estimates were prepared and work started. The outbreak of war stopped further progress for the time being, but a prototype locomotive was built and tested on the Manchester-Altrincham line in 1941. A large amount of equipment had been manufactured and this was put into store until after the war. Work was resumed in 1949 and all the lines included in the scheme were opened for electric working on 14 September 1954. They comprised the main line between Manchester and Sheffield, with a branch from Penistone to the marshalling yards at Wath: a total of 68 route-miles.

For mixed traffic working 58 Bo-Bo 1,868hp locomotives were built in 1950, with nose-suspended Metropolitan-Vickers 467hp traction motors, which were substantially the same as the prototype. They became Class 76. Later, seven Co-Co 2,490hp passenger locomotives were added in 1954, with Metropolitan-Vickers 415hp nose-suspended traction motors. The maximum speed of the former locomotives was 65 mile/h and of the latter 90 mile/h. Names were given to 13 of the mixed traffic locomotives. The prototype had been loaned to the Netherlands Railways from 1947 to 1952, and the Dutch drivers named it *Tommy*. This name was retained, but the others were called after the gods and heroes of Greek mythology. Similar names were given to the seven passenger locomotives.

The Manchester-Sheffield electrification has unfortunately fallen on evil days. Electric passenger trains no longer run, except for links between Manchester, Hatfield and Glossop; otherwise only freight trains now take their power from the conductor wires of the old Great Central route between the two cities. The seven passenger locomotives have been sold to the Netherlands State Railways, and all Manchester-Sheffield passenger trains are diesel-operated over the old Midland line via Chinley. Much of the electric equipment is now getting old and needs replacement, and at the time of writing it appears that even the continuation of electric freight haulage is threatened.

25kV 50Hz ac Electrification

As described in Chapter 1, the adoption of 25kV 50Hz ac electrification was due to the vision of R. A. Riddles when Member of the Railway Executive for Mechanical and Electrical Engineering. His plea for the electrification of the main lines was turned down, as we have seen, in favour of dieselisation. The Modernisation Plan did indeed pay lip service to electrification but limited it to suburban lines. In 1956 Riddles was justified, because the system he had recommended was adopted as the standard for British Railways.

Although, unlike diesel traction, the principles and problems of electric traction were well understood at the time the railways were Nationalised, electrification at 25kV 50Hz ac posed special difficulties. New design had to be developed for almost every item of equipment. Foreign designs could not be adopted indiscriminately because conditions in the United Kingdom differed so widely from those in other countries.[13]

When the LMR scheme was authorised it was proposed that certain sections with limited clearance (ie under 11in) would have to be electrified at the lower kilovoltage of 6.25. However, tests showed that the clearance necessary was not as great as had at first been thought, and by reducing the height of the loading gauge from 13ft 6in to 13ft 1in it was possible to electrify the whole route at 25kV.

The advantages of overhead construction at 25kV ac instead of 1,500V dc were considerable. On the Manchester-Sheffield electrification there are substations every six miles, whereas the 25kV scheme would need substations only about every 32 miles. Furthermore, a dc substation needs transformers, rectifiers, control gear, circuit breakers, and switchgear in an enclosed building; whereas an ac substation only requires a transformer, circuit breakers, and switchgear, and everything can be out of doors. Then again, there are savings in the cross sections of the overhead wires, because the higher the voltage the smaller the amount of current necessary for the same power. The savings on this account can be as high as 25%.[14]

The overhead wires consist basically of a catenary wire from which is suspended by dropper wires at appropriate intervals the contact wire from which the locomotive or multiple-unit draws its supply. This is known as 'simple catenary equipment', and all the wires mentioned of course carry current. A difficulty arises with a simple catenary, in that, in the middle of the span between the supporting structures, the locomotive's pantograph will lift the normally level contact wire. The pantograph is therefore moving up and down, and this movement at high speeds will be very rapid, with the consequent risk that the pantograph, by not moving fast enough, will lose contact with the wire. This difficulty, it was thought, could be overcome by making the contact wire as flexible at the structures as it is in the middle of the span. A so-called 'stitch' was therefore inserted at each supporting structure. A stitch wire is connected to the catenary wire a short distance each side of every support, so by-passing the fixed connection at a support, and from the stitch wire there are droppers to the contact wire. Since the contact wire is now flexible throughout its length, the upward movement of the contact wire is lessened. It was proposed that a stitched catenary should be erected on all routes where speeds were to exceed 60 mile/h.

However, it is not easy to get the correct tension on a stitch wire, and for this reason the 'compound catenary' is more popular. In this form of construction an auxiliary catenary wire is suspended from the catenary proper by droppers, and from the auxiliary cantenary other droppers support the contact wire. It can perhaps be regarded as making the stitch wire continuous. It was introduced on all lines with a maximum speed of 100 mile/h which were brought into service before 1966. It is a very satisfactory method, but it is expensive. A much simpler solution was subsequently found in the 'sagged simple cantenary', in which the contact wire is allowed to sag between the supports instead of being level. The sag in the centre of a span of 75yd is about 4in. This has the effect of reducing the vertical movement of the pantograph and gives good current collection at speeds well over 100 mile/h. It was therefore adopted for the Weaver Junction-Glasgow electrification, and with its introduction came much lighter and more unobtrusive supporting structures.[15] (Riddles, who had expected these from the start, had criticised the massive structures used on the earlier electrification).[16]

Locomotives for the ac electrification

It was established first in France, after tests, that ac locomotives with tap-changing equipment for the transformers and dc traction motors connected permanently in parallel, offered considerable advantages. There is much greater smoothness of control than on dc locomotives which use notching through series resistances and transition of the motors from series to parallel. Indeed, as a result of their investigations, French Railways rates ac locomotives, equipped with dc motors supplied by rectifiers, as capable of hauling loads 60% heavier than those within the capacity of the latest types of dc locomotives of the same weight.[17]

It was not however till the 1950s that rectifiers were developed, sufficiently robust and reliable for traction, to enable dc motors to be used on ac electric locomotives. The first rectifiers were of the mercury arc type, but they were soon followed by both germanium and silicon semiconductors with electro-mechanical tap-changers for voltage control.[18]

For the Euston to Liverpool and Manchester scheme, 200 locomotives were built in six main classes. Of these the first 100 were of five different designs, to meet a specification requiring the haulage of 475 ton passenger trains at speeds of up to 100 mile/h, and 950 ton freight trains at an average of 42 mile/h, with a maximum of 55 mile/h. They were to be of the Bo-Bo type and, as the Chief Civil Engineer had stipulated a maximum axle load of 20 tons, this limited the total weight to 80 tons. To reduce unsprung weight on the axles to a minimum, flexible drive was required.[19]

The first 60 locomotives (Classes AL1-4) were fitted with mercury-arc rectifiers, but the remaining 40 (Class AL5) had semiconductor rectifiers and rheostatic braking.[20] (At the time that the first locomotives were ordered semiconductor rectifiers were comparatively new, and, although they were performing satisfactorily, it was thought safer to fit the customary mercury-arc rectifiers. However, water-cooled mercury arc rectifiers are difficult to maintain and not very reliable; so there were second thoughts when the AL5s came to be built and AEI germanium or silicon rectifiers were fitted instead.)[21]

The five classes, together with their later British Railways numerical classifications, were:

AL1 (Class 81):
AEI (British Thomson-Houston); 3,300hp; four AEI (BTH) springborne dc, traction motors driving through Alsthom quill drive; 23 locomotives.
AL2 (Class 82):
AEI (Metropolitan-Vickers); 3,300hp; four AEI (MV) dc traction motors driving through Alsthom quill drive; 10 locomotives.
AL3 (Class 83):
English Electric; 2,950hp; four English Electric springborne dc traction motors driving through SLM resilient drive; 12 locomotives.
AL4 (Class 84):
General Electric; 3,000hp; four GEC springborne dc traction motors driving through Brown Boveri spring drive; 10 locomotives.
AL5 (Class 85):
British Railways; 3,300hp; four AEI (BTH) dc traction motors driving through Alsthom quill drive; 40 locomotives.

The first of the second batch of 100 locomotives (Type AL6 and later Class 86) made their appearance in 1965, five years later than AL1-4. They embodied many alterations in the light of experience with the earlier locomotives, though the wheel arrangement and weight were the same. They were built by British Railways and English Electric's Vulcan Foundry. They had four AEI traction motors, delivering a total of 3,600hp, but these were axle-hung, nose-suspended, to avoid the complication and expense of flexible drives. They had only one pantograph, as experience with the earlier locomotives had shown that only one was necessary. The AL6 is a particularly reliable locomotive, but there is considerable unsprung weight owing to the axle-hung traction motors, and the type of bogie fitted caused poor vertical riding at high speed.[22] Indeed, Types AL1 and AL5, which had bogies of the same fundamental design, suffered similarly, although this type of bogie stood up well to 100 mile/h running. The dampers became ineffective after a low mileage, and to overcome this improved dampers were fitted. Further investigations resulted in the greater proportion of the AL6s being modified in 1972 to incorporate a new bogie suspension that gave greatly improved riding. Locomotives thus modified are designated Class 86/2.[23]

Experience with the AL6s resulted in a reversion to flexible suspension of the traction motors, with a view to advancing the maximum speed to 125 mile/h.[24] The first of these new AL7 or Class 87 locomotives appeared in 1973. They had four frame-mounted GEC 1,250hp traction motors and a flexible drive. Their total hp of 5,000 makes them the most powerful locomotives to run in Great Britain. They ride excellently. All 36 have been given names, which are reminiscent of LNWR naming practice, and many of the modified 86s have also been named.

The latest development to affect electric locomotive

design is the use of thyristors, with which, at the time of writing, one Class 87 locomotive has been fitted by GEC Traction. With these controlled rectifiers it is possible to eliminate the normal electro-mechanical tap-changer, and thereby improve performance, whilst reducing maintenance and weight.

A thyristor is a unidirectional electrical switch without any moving parts. It is a semiconductor with the valuable attribute that it can be used to determine the instant at which conduction begins. Alone, or in conjunction with other thyristors, it can switch from small powers up to many thousands of kilowatts. A special characteristic of a thyristor is its 'gate'. When a small current flows between this gate and the cathode (negative) of the thyristor, it causes an electric current to pass from cathode to anode (positive), thus switching the thyristor into its conducting mode. Once this power current has been started, the gate cannot by itself make it stop. In ac systems, however, this occurs naturally every half-cycle when there is a current zero. The thyristor controls the mean voltage applied to other equipments by advancing or delaying the point in the voltage cycle at which it is switched on. The advantage gained from thyristors is that they improve performance because of the flexibility of electronic control systems. The voltage applied to a dc traction motor from an ac supply is normally varied by a series of taps on the supply transformer, the lower voltage so obtained being rectified before being applied to the motors. The simplest method of introducing thyristor control is to replace the rectifiers by thyristors and dispense with the tap-changer and taps on the supply transformer. It is then possible to control a traction motor armature and field independently, which can provide automatic wheel-slip correction and allow a locomotive to be worked much closer to the adhesion limit. It is claimed that this gives an increase of 25% in haulage capacity. In the scheme applied to the thyristor-fitted Class 87 locomotive, the voltage applied to the traction motors armatures is gradually increased by advancing the firing angles of the thyristors.[25]

Multiple-units

All the passenger traffic on the Great Eastern line, the Great Northern line, the Glasgow suburban network, and the suburban and short distance ac routes of the London Midland Region is operated by multiple-unit trains. The Liverpool Street-Shenfield-Southend-Chelmsford lines were electrified at 1,500V dc in 1949. These had to be converted to 50Hz ac and new equipment provided for 124 trains. As regards completely new multiple-unit sets, a total of 361 were needed for the above electric services (excluding the Great Northern section, which was electrified later). On both the Great Eastern and Scottish lines certain sections were electrified at 6.25kV because of the difficulty of getting the clearances originally stipulated for 25kV.[26]

Perhaps the most noteworthy amongst the earlier multiple-unit trains were the 23 sets for the Clacton express service. They comprised eight 4-car units (each with a griddle refreshment car), seven 4-car units (without griddle cars), and eight 2-car units. The peak operating formation was a 10-car train from Liverpool Street to Thorpe-le-Soken, where it was divided into a 6-car portion for Clacton and a 4-car unit for Walton. Current is collected by a Stone-Faiveley type pantograph and, through an air blast breaker, it passes to the changeover switch that connects the four sections of the transformer primary winding in series for 25kV supply and in parallel for 6.25kV. On the secondary winding there are four equal voltage tappings which are selected in turn by an air-operated camshaft tap-changer and which provide the major voltage steps. For intertapping there is a resistor which is cut out progressively, so that there are 20 notches in the acceleration sequence.[27]

For the later GN electrification of 1975 there are some most interesting inner suburban 3-car units which normally take their current from the overhead 25kV supply, but in the tunnel sections they collect it from a third-rail at 750V dc.

At the time of writing, the most momentous of all electric sets, the Advanced Passenger Train, is shortly to undergo its trials.

NOTES

1 Goldsack, Paul J. (Ed); *Jane's World Railways;* Macdonald & Jane's, 1978, p492
2 ibid, Foreword
3 ibid, p492
4 McGuigan, J. H.; *The Giant's Causeway Tramway;* The Oakwood Press, 1964
5 Institution of Electrical Engineers, *Conference on Performance of Electrified Railways,* October 1968; W. J. A. Sykes, '750V Third Rail Electrification on British Railways' pp9-10
6 Klapper, C. F.; *Sir Herbert Walker's Southern Railway;* Ian Allan, 1973, p49
7 Sykes, op cit, p210
8 ibid, pp213-4
9 Jarvis, R. G.; Information to the Author
10 Sykes, op cit, pp213-4
11 Jarvis, op cit
12 Sykes, op cit, pp210, 224-5
13 Chief Electrical Engineer, BR Central Staff, *50 Cycle ac Electrification: Progress Report on Design,* 6 September 1957
14 British Insulated Callender's Cables, *Overhead Equipment for 25kV 50 Cycle ac Railway Electrification,* December 1957
15 ibid; Nock, O. S.; *Electric: Euston to Glasgow;* Ian Allan Ltd, 1974, pp.86,88
16 Riddles, R. A.; Information to the Author
17 BICC, op cit
18 GEC Traction Ltd, *Electric Locomotives*
19 IEE *Conference,* op cit, A. H. Emerson, 'Main Line 25kV 50Hz ac, Electrification on London Midland Region of British Rail', pp.121-3
20 ibid
21 ibid
22 Nock, op cit, p93
23 Emerson, op cit, p141
24 ibid, p133
25 GEC Traction, op cit, C. E. Band, *Power Electronics in ac and dc Traction Systems,* GEC Traction Ltd
26 IEE *Conference,* op cit, C. M. S. Maguire, 'The Suburban Aspects of British Rail 25kV ac, Electrification', p163, Nock, O. S.; *Britain's New Railway;* Ian Allan Ltd, 1966, pp48-9
27 Maguire, op cit, p193

Right: Modern electrified main line: Class 87 No 87.019 takes the 13.45 Euston-Glasgow through the cutting north of Watford Junction in June 1976./*Brian Morrison*

Below: On the West Coast main line electrification near Tring, an overhead line maintenance train at work in the late 1960s./*BR*

Top left: The run-up to 25kV electrification came in the form of the 1,500V dc Manchester-Sheffield-Wath scheme completed in the mid-1950s. One of the MSW Bo-Bos, No 26002, at Ilford car depot, on Great Eastern territory, ready to work a test train to Shenfield on 12 November 1950./*C.C.B. Herbert*

The big Southern dc third-trail schemes of postwar years exemplified by Kent Coast Phase 1 emu stock *(left)* at Faversham, bound for Victoria; and *(below left)* a 12-car formation of Bournemouth fast stock, power unit 4REP No 3001 leading, on a crew training run from Basingstoke Bournemouth near Shawford Junction in March 1967./*P.J. Sharpe; John H. Bird*

Southern Region electric and electro-diesel power. *Above:* A class 71, No E5023, ready to depart from Victoria with the 'Golden Arrow'. *Below:* One of the ill-starred Class 74s on a Weymouth Quay-Waterloo boat train near Clapham Junction in 1973./*Brian E. Morrison*

Above left: Class 73 No 73.142 promoted to higher things with a Royal Train to Southampton Docks on 8 August 1979, ready to depart from Waterloo. */John Scrace*

Centre left: At Guide Bridge, on the MSW electrification, one of the passenger locomotives takes over the Liverpool-Harwich boat train from steam haulage in the late 1950s. */Kenneth Field*

Below: The Colchester-Clacton 25kV ac 'test-bed' with the car depot and men at work outside Clacton station in early 1959./*BR*

Right: The first of the 25kV ac production locomotives, No E3001, on the Styal Loop in late 1959./*BR*

Below right: Manchester Piccadilly in March 1961, with AEI (Rugby) 25kV ac locomotive No E3011 (left) and GEC locomotive No E3044(right)./*D. Kingston*

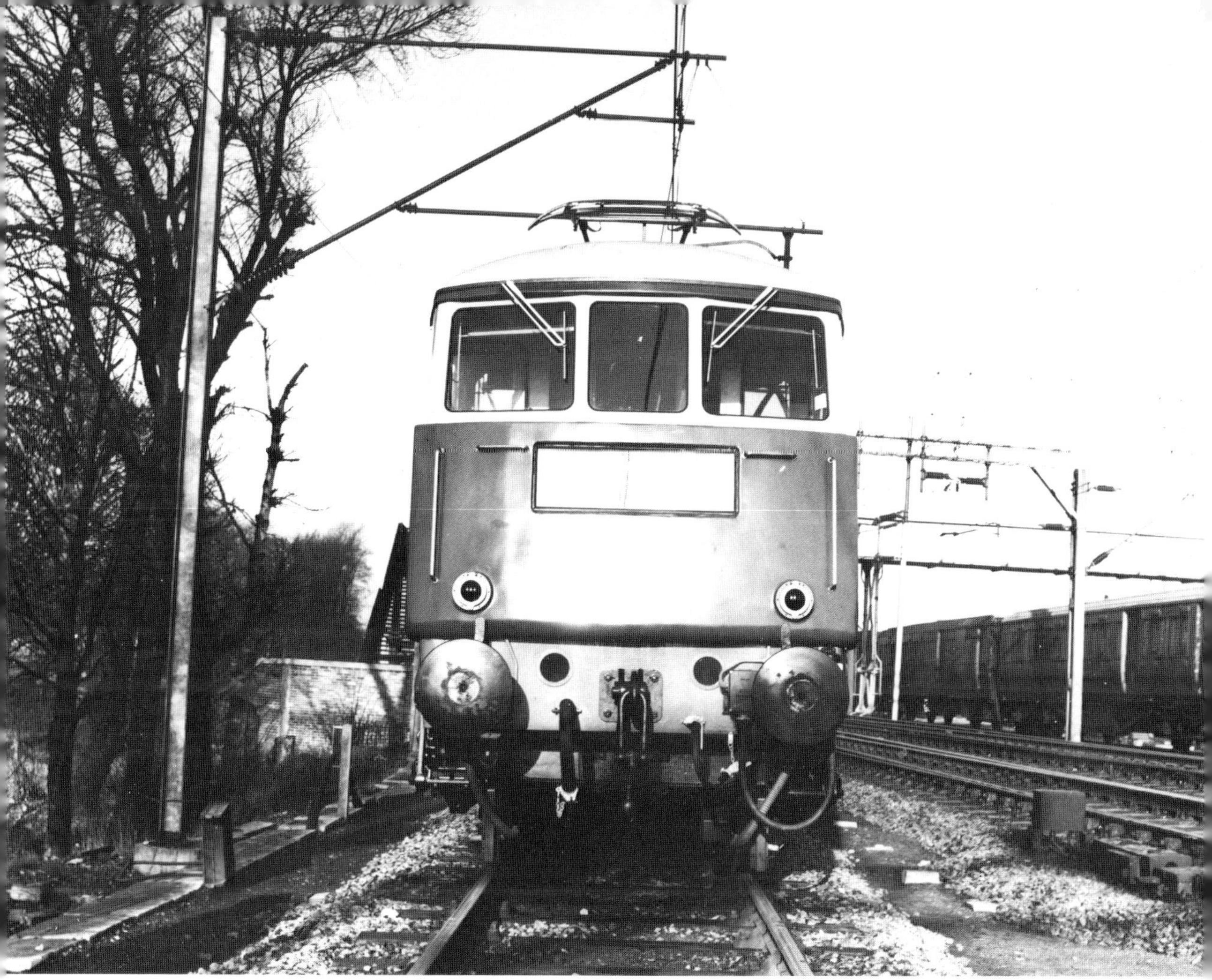

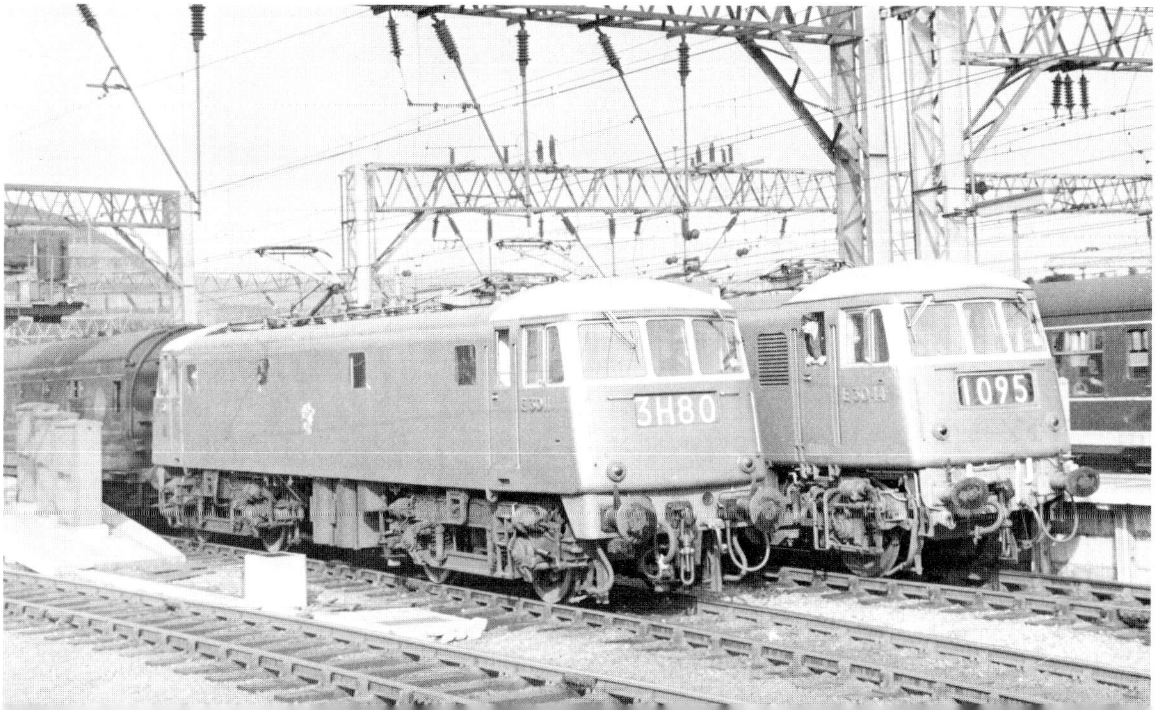
3H80
1095

Top left: Manchester Piccadilly in September 1960, the occasion of the first big press visit to inspect 25kV ac electrification between Crewe and Manchester./*GEC*

Above left: 25kV ac electrification equipment line-up – at Battersea Yard, SR, of all places. Two types of multiple-unit power cars and three locomotives on display./*W.H.R. Godwin*

Left: The transductor 25kV ac locomotive built by English Electric, No E3100, heads an unusual test train on the Crewe-Manchester line in the early 1960s. No E3100 was an important step in the evolution of thyristor controlled equipment./*GEC*

Above: Two of the Clacton express service 25kV ac emus pass a dmu at Colchester, and slow for the station stop with a Clacton-Liverpool St train in May 1977./*Brian E. Morrison*

Right: Latest electrification – the Scottish Region's Argyle Line making use of the Glasgow Central Low Level line. The Class 314 units have thyristor equipment.

Postscript

The transition from steam operation on British Railways has long since been completed, but transition in another form continues. As R. A. Riddles foresaw, the future must lie in electrification; and the expansion of this form of motive power, at the expense of diesel, is likely to be accelerated on account of the increasing shortage and increasing cost of oil fuel. A future generation of railwaymen may indeed look back with surprise at the haste with which new steam locomotives were hustled to the scrap yard to make way for such a massive expenditure on diesel power as to delay the electrification of most of the main lines for decades.

Modern motive power has been accompanied by faster services, cleaner working conditions, greater flexibility in operation, and greater comfort for train crews. But much has been lost in the process: the majestic beauty of the steam locomotive has been replaced by the box-like exterior of the diesel or electric locomotive; instead of the colourful liveries and armorial achievements of the great companies there is the dinginess of rail blue and the drab double arrow totem; and the romantic great trains of the past have given away to the slug-like contours of the High Speed Train. Nevertheless, it has at last been realised how much of the glamour has departed from the railways, for increasing numbers of electric and diesel locomotives are being named, and the enthusiasm raised by private ventures in steam traction has led to British Railways running steam-hauled trains of their own.

It is difficult to believe that diesel or electric locomotives and multiple-unit trains will ever inspire the affection with which the great steam engines have been regarded by railwaymen and amateur enthusiasts alike. Recently, Riddles had his first ride in the cab of a Class 87 electric locomotive. I asked him what it was like. 'I didn't really notice,' he replied, 'The driver was an old steam man and we talked about steam engines all the time.'

Left: Goodbye to all that – the early sunshine at Holbeck mpd, Leeds./*Eric Treacy*

Above: Two 'Deltics', No D9001 *St Paddy* trailing, en route to Vulcan Foundry for attention in 1961, seen here at Cross Lane, Manchester./*J.R. Carter*

Right: Front end of 25kV ac locomotive No E3041./*Sam Lambert*

Left: Front end of BR/Sulzer 1Co-Co1 diesel-electric locomotive. /*Sam Lambert*

Above: V2s Nos 60961 and 60939 at York mpd in October 1964. /*Brian Stephenson*

Below: Steam for the future – restored 'Jubilee' 4-6-0 No 5690 *Leander* departs from Carnforth with the down 'Cumbrian Coast Express' on 31 May 1979./*J.H. Cooper-Smith*

An Inter-City 125 leaves Kings Cross with the 17.00 for Edinburgh in September 1978.
/*Brian C. Morrison*

254 018

Index